# P–K4* ANYONE?

Excellent . . . but where do you go from there?

Fred Reinfeld, world-famous chess master and teacher, has stated, "It is relatively simple to learn a few brilliant openings. But then the average player flounders pointlessly, throwing away moves because he has **no clear idea of what he is trying to achieve.**"

In this unique book Mr. Reinfeld, synthesizing a lifetime of chess experience, begins by demonstrating **the bold endgame patterns that insure resounding victories.**

Every move then becomes a calculated step toward a decisive checkmate. You will soon master the slashing attacks of the International Champions and be well on your way toward **WINNING CHESS**

* P—K4: pawn moves to the 4th space in the King's file. For a complete explanation of chess notation, see pages 36-41.

D0038059

# HOW TO PLAY
# WINNING CHESS

# BY FRED REINFELD

BANTAM BOOKS • NEW YORK

HOW TO PLAY WINNING CHESS

*A Bantam Reference Library edition / published December 1962*
*2nd printing ... December 1962*      *7th printing .... August 1965*
*3rd printing ....... June 1964*      *8th printing ..... March 1969*
*4th printing ..... August 1965*      *9th printing .... August 1970*
*5th printing .. September 1966*      *10th printing ....... June 1971*
*6th printing ..... October 1967*     *11th printing ....... May 1972*
*12th printing*
*13th printing*
*14th printing*
*15th printing*
*16th printing*
*17th printing*

*Cover illustration courtesy of the Carlebach Galleries*

*Library of Congress Catalog Card Number: 62-20943*

*Published simultaneously in the United States and Canada*

*Bantam Books are published by Bantam Books, Inc., a National*
*General company. Its trade-mark, consisting of the words "Bantam*
*Books" and the portrayal of a bantam, is registered in the United*
*States Patent Office and in other countries. Marca Registrada.*
*Bantam Books, Inc., 666 Fifth Avenue, New York, N.Y. 10019.*

PRINTED IN THE UNITED STATES OF AMERICA

# CONTENTS

# INTRODUCTION

Chess is perhaps the oldest and certainly the most popular game in the world.

The ablest historians of the game place its origins in India about 600 A.D. From India the game spread in all directions. The westward migration, by way of the Arab incursions of medieval times, eventually reached Europe.

During the Middle Ages chess was the great leisure-time activity of the aristocratic and wealthy classes. A knowledge of chess was considered one of the prime social graces of every "parfit and gentil" knight. One reason for this, of course, was the obvious connection between war and chess. In ancient India the pieces had included chariots, elephants, horses, and infantry—all these features pointing clearly to the military inspiration of the game.

The Arabs were the first to develop a systematic chess literature, even if it was only in the form of manuscripts. Their best players wrote treatises on the game, demonstrating what they considered the best opening moves and the most useful winning methods. They also published collections of beautiful problems.

There was keen rivalry among the best players, for an exceptional degree of skill at chess was greatly esteemed among the Arabs. They also fostered blindfold play, which is rather surprising in view of their difficulties with a standard chess notation, or method of recording moves. From all indications, they were deeply sensitive to the solace that chess can offer. There is a famous passage, for example, in a poem written by al-Mutamid in the eleventh century in which he observes that "chess yields us, when we need them most, companions for our loneliness."

The progress of chess in the Arab regions was held back to some extent by Mohammedan theologians who held that it was nothing more than a sinful pastime. Curiously enough, when chess became popular in Europe the Church took the same attitude, probably because many games must have been the subject of a wager.

In Europe the game made tremendous strides. The powers of some pieces were increased, making the play much more lively and therefore more popular. The number of works on chess increased considerably. (It remains true even today that the number of books devoted to chess is more extensive than that devoted to all other games put together.)

It was the invention of the printing press that really gave the spread of chess playing enormous impetus. Treatises and manuals on the game could now be produced in quantity, multiplying the number of readers and players. The growth of great cities and the improvement of communications also favored this trend. The coffeehouses of London and the cafés of Paris became famous haunts for chess players. In Paris, for example, Voltaire, Rousseau, Diderot, and the young Bonaparte were all passionate if not particularly skillful devotees of the game.

With the coming of the eighteenth century we have the emergence of really great players. The first of these, François André Philidor (1726-1795) was primarily an operatic composer and only secondarily a chess player. Yet he was universally recognized as the greatest master of his age. Philidor's manual on the game was the best of its kind and remained in demand for a century. Today it is of course merely a curiosity, but it is still notable for its emphasis on Pawn play—a pioneering concept in Philidor's day. It was Philidor who started the rage for blindfold play which was later to be developed to a phenomenal degree.

After Philidor's death the two leading chess-playing countries were England and France. The sharp rivalry between these countries reached a climax in 1834 in the match between Alexander McDonnell (1798-1835) and Louis Charles Mahé de Labourdonnais (1795-1840). The Homeric struggle between them lasted 84 games, winding up in a convincing victory for Labourdonnais, with 44 wins, 27 losses, and 13 draws.

To appreciate the arduous nature of this match we must remember that it was played without clocks—that is, without a time limit. Both men were accustomed to move slowly, McDonnell often taking up to forty-five minutes to ponder a single move. Yet there is no trace of this in the games, which abound in sparkling and inspired moves.

With the passage of only a few years England and France were represented by new champions. The leading English player was Howard Staunton (1810-1874); the French champion was Pierre Charles Fournier de Saint-Amant (1800-1873). Staunton, one of the outstanding Shakespearean scholars of his time, was a sound if rather phlegmatic player. He made a lasting contribution to chess literature with his famous *Handbook,* which first appeared in 1847 and has since gone through innumerable editions. Saint-Amant was similarly sound and colorless. The meeting of these two players in 1843 left no doubt of Staunton's superiority (11 wins, 6 losses, and 4 draws).

But the pompous and irascible Staunton was not destined to enjoy his triumph for very long. Germany was now beginning to produce great players. These included a group of seven brilliant Berlin masters known as "the seven Pleiades." During the 1840's they started one of the earliest chess magazines—the *Deutsche Schachzeitung,* now the oldest chess magazine in existence. But the greatest German master of this period was Adolf Anderssen (1818-1879), a mild-mannered Breslau schoolmaster.

Anderssen's approach to the game was quite different from that of Staunton. From the very first move on, Anderssen sought complications and lively combinations and attacks. At a time when chess threatened to become dull, Anderssen reestablished it as a spirited struggle. In the first international tournament ever held (London, 1851), Anderssen won the first prize in very superior style, leaving Staunton far behind.

Although Anderssen's active playing career was destined to span another twenty-five years, it did not take long for him to be toppled from his pre-eminent position. His successful rival came from a country which had so far failed to distinguish itself in master chess—the United States. Though his participation in master play lasted only about three years, Paul Morphy (1837-1884) became the most famous player in the history of the game.

Morphy was just as brilliant as Anderssen, but in addition he had a revolutionary idea that made him the superior of all his contemporaries: Morphy was the first to insist on rapid, effective development of the pieces in the opening stage. This gave him a "secret weapon" that helped him defeat his opponents with the greatest of ease. Even Anderssen, for all his genius, could put up only feeble resistance against Morphy. In their match at Paris in 1858, Morphy won 7 games, lost 2, and drew 2. Thus the triumph of Morphy's ideas was emphatically documented, so that he is generally considered the first though unofficial World Champion.

Morphy was less interested in chess than in the law, which was his chosen profession. Two years after his match with Anderssen he disappeared permanently from the world of chess. Yet his ideas had made a lasting impression. His combination of quick development and brilliant attack became the rage in master chess.

One of the finest of the young masters who followed in Morphy's footsteps was Wilhelm Steinitz (1836-1900); born in Prague, Steinitz moved on to Vienna, then to London, and spent his last seventeen years in the United States. After Morphy's disappearance from international competition, it soon became clear that Anderssen and Steinitz were the two leading masters of the day. Their match in London in 1866 was a surprise to Anderssen's admirers, who thought that the older, more experienced man would have a very easy time of it. In an extremely hard-fought struggle of 14 games Steinitz won by 8-6, with no games drawn.

Steinitz was now recognized, though not universally, as World Champion. As time went on his title took on a more official character. His match victories against the Englishman, Blackburne, the German, Zukertort, and the Russian, Tchigorin, left no doubt of his supremacy, which lasted until 1894.

Steinitz's lengthy reign completely revolutionized chess. Even during his match with Anderssen it had become clear that his style of play was in a transitional phase. Instead of playing wholeheartedly for attack, he often resorted to sober defensive play which at the time was a novelty. Gradually the revolutionary nature of Steinitz's ideas was revealed in his games and newspaper columns.

Steinitz had broken definitely with the old easygoing idea of sacrificing material in the hope of a winning attack. He insisted stubbornly on the validity of the defense, with the idea of winning in the endgame with the extra material amassed in the earlier stages. The right method, he preached tirelessly, was to forego speculative attacks and build up small positional advantages by judicious improvement of one's position.

For a long time Steinitz was ridiculed and reviled, but his stubborn advocacy of his novel ideas over a period of three decades eventually had its effect, especially on the younger generation. The result has been that every modern master has been influenced in greater or lesser degree by the Steinitzian theories.

It would take us too far afield to follow chess history since Steinitz's day in full detail. Chess tournaments and matches became much more frequent. Many outstanding new masters appeared. Chess clubs, chess columns in newspapers, and chess magazines multiplied and flourished. A few words are in order about the World Champions who reigned after Steinitz.

Steinitz was finally dethroned in 1894 by Dr. Emanuel Lasker, who in turn held the title till 1921. Lasker's approach to chess was paradoxical. Though a self-proclaimed disciple of Steinitz, Lasker was above all a fighter. He took risks, his play was sometimes spotty; he viewed chess as a personal struggle and he tried to exploit the temperament of his opponents. In an age when the triumph of dry technique threatened to engulf master chess, Lasker remained an inspiring maverick who went his own way.

But even Lasker had to admit defeat eventually—by the much younger José Raoul Capablanca. This Cuban master seemed in his youth to be the very epitome of flawless technique. But as he grew older the aura of perfection deserted him. After defeating Lasker in 1921, he lost his title only six years later to Alexander Alekhine, a master of a vastly different stamp.

Alekhine was one of the great towering geniuses of the game—perhaps the greatest of all. What is especially impressive about him is his versatility. He was a superb tactician —inventive, imaginative, full of inexhaustible resources. But he was also an outstanding technician who could beat every master at his own style. And he poured into his games his own inexhaustible vitality.

In 1935, Alekhine seemed to be through when he lost his title by a narrow margin to the Dutch master Dr. Max Euwe. But two years later he decisively defeated Euwe to regain his cherished title. Thereafter he reigned undefeated until his tragically premature death in 1946.

Alekhine's death gave the International Chess Federation an opportunity to take official control of the matches for the world title. This was an important step forward, as the federation arranged for far more frequent matches for the title and thus enormously increased interest in the game.

Since Alekhine's death all the World Champions have been players from the U.S.S.R.—Mikhail Botvinnik, Vassily Smyslov, and Mikhail Tal. At this writing Botvinnik holds the title.

Over the course of many centuries chess has made enormous progress. It is more popular today than ever before, a hobby which, in my opinion, is second to none. This introduction to the "royal game" has been written in the hope that it will contribute to the widespread popularity of this most ancient and yet most modern of all games.

# 1

# THE ELEMENTS

Chess, the world's most popular game, is played by two opponents on a chessboard of 64 squares.

These squares are divided into 8 vertical rows (known as "files") and 8 horizontal rows (known as "ranks").

Every square on the board is used, and, as you will see later, each one has its own special name. To make it easier to distinguish one square from another, they are alternately colored light and dark. We always refer to the light squares as "white squares" and to the dark squares as "black squares."

BLACK

WHITE

DIAGRAM 1
The chessboard, with its 8 files and 8 ranks, making up 64 alternately colored squares.

The board should be placed in such a way that the right-hand corner square nearest each player is a white square.

## THE STARTING POSITION

The players begin with an equal number of men on each side: 16. The chessmen come in two colors—White has the light-colored ones, and Black has the dark-colored ones. The names of these men are as follows:

| WHITE | | BLACK |
|:---:|:---:|:---:|
| ♔ | 1 King | ♚ |
| ♕ | 1 Queen | ♛ |
| ♖ | 2 Rooks | ♜ |
| ♗ | 2 Bishops | ♝ |
| ♘ | 2 Knights | ♞ |
| ♙ | 8 Pawns | ♟ |

Diagram 2 shows how these men are set up at the beginning of the game.

DIAGRAM 2
The starting position, with a white square at the right-hand corner nearest each player.

Note that Black's forces are always at the top of the diagram, while White's are at the bottom. It's easy to memorize the placement of the men:

The Rooks go at the corners. Next to them are the Knights. Then come the Bishops. Finally, the King and Queen are placed on the middle squares of the first row, or rank.

The White Queen and the Black Queen face each other across the Queen file. (Each file is named for the piece that stands on it at the beginning of the game.)

Remember the rule of "Queen on her own color." The White Queen is placed on a white square, the Black Queen on a black square.

On the other hand, while the two Kings similarly face each other along the King file, you will find that the White King is placed on a black square, while the Black King is placed on a white square. Check these comments with Diagram 2 and with the position of your men on your own board.

The Bishop next to the King is known as the "King Bishop." The file on which the White and Black King Bishops are placed is the King Bishop file.

Next to the King Bishop is the King Knight, on the King Knight file. Then comes the King Rook, on the King Rook file.

Similarly we have on the other side the Queen Bishop, Queen Knight, and Queen Rook. These are placed, respectively, on the Queen Bishop, Queen Knight, and Queen Rook files.

White's Pawns are posted on White's second rank, while Black's Pawns go on Black's second rank. Each Pawn is named for the file on which it stands. For example, the Pawn on the King file (in front of the King) is the King Pawn.

## HOW THE CHESSMEN MOVE

Before we consider how each chessman moves, there are some things we need to know about moves in general.

The game always starts with a move by White. Thereafter the players take turns in making their moves. Only one move can be made at a time. Only one chessman can occupy a square at a time.

With one exception, only one chessman can be moved at one time. The exception, known as "castling" (pp. 27-32), allows a player to move his King and a Rook—all in one move.

All chessmen have the power of capturing. An enemy chessman is captured by removing it from its square and replacing it with one of your own chessmen—*on the same square.* All the chessmen capture the same way they move; the only exception is the Pawn.

## THE KING

The King is the most valuable piece in chess, but its moving and capturing powers are rather limited.

BLACK

WHITE

DIAGRAM 3
How the King moves.

The King's moving powers are shown in Diagram 3. The King can move to any of the squares marked with an arrow. The King can move one square in any direction—vertically, horizontally, or diagonally. (By a diagonal we mean a row of squares of the same color, which touch each other only at the corners. In Diagram 3, any King move to a white square would be a diagonal move.)

The King captures the same way he moves. He captures by replacing the enemy chessman which has been removed from its square.

BLACK

WHITE

DIAGRAM 4a
White's King can capture the Black Pawn (horizontal capture) or the Black Knight (diagonal capture).

For reasons that will be explained later on, the King can never move to a square—or capture on a square—that is within the capturing range of an enemy chessman. It follows that the White King and Black King will never be found on adjoining squares.

DIAGRAM 4b
White's King has captured the Black Knight (see Diagram 4a).

## THE QUEEN

Like the King, the Queen can move in any direction—horizontally, vertically, or diagonally. But there is a vast difference in their powers, as the Queen is the strongest piece on the board. She can move to any empty square along an unobstructed file, rank, or diagonal that is accessible to the square on which she is placed. See Diagram 5.

DIAGRAM 5
The Queen can move to any of the squares marked with an arrow.

Only two kinds of obstacles can hold up the Queen's progress along a line. One is the presence of a friendly chessman. This effectively blocks the line, as the Queen cannot leap over it or displace it.

The other obstacle is an enemy chessman. The Queen cannot leap over it, but she can capture it by displacement.

Of course the Queen can go in only one direction at a time, and can make only one capture at a time. Diagram 6a shows the Queen's moving and capturing powers.

BLACK

WHITE

DIAGRAM 6a
White's Queen has a choice of capturing the Black Bishop or Rook or Pawn. Note how the presence of the White Rook obstructs one of the Queen's diagonals.

BLACK

WHITE

DIAGRAM 6b
White's Queen has captured the Black Rook (see Diagram 6a).

## THE ROOK

After the Queen, the Rook is the next strongest piece. It can move vertically or horizontally—one direction at a time— like the Queen. But unlike the Queen, the Rook cannot move diagonally.

DIAGRAM 7
The Rook can move to any of the squares marked with an arrow (compare with Diagram 5).

The Rook captures by displacement of enemy forces. The Rook cannot leap over or displace one of its own men.

DIAGRAM 8a
The White Rook can capture the Black Queen or Knight. It cannot capture the Black Pawn because it cannot move diagonally. Nor can the Rook capture the Black Bishop, because its path is blocked by the White Knight.

BLACK

WHITE

DIAGRAM 8b
White's Rook has
captured the Black
Queen (see Diagram
8a).

## THE BISHOP

The Bishop moves only diagonally. It cannot make vertical or horizontal moves. It moves in only one direction at a time.

Because a Bishop moves only on diagonals, it is confined to squares of the same color. A Bishop placed on a white square at the beginning of the game can move and capture only on white squares. Similarly, a black-squared Bishop can move and capture only on black squares.

BLACK

WHITE

DIAGRAM 9
The Bishop can move
to any of the squares
marked with an arrow.

The Bishop captures the same way it moves—on diagonals. It captures enemy chessmen by displacing them from their squares. It cannot displace any of its own pieces, and it cannot leap over any chessman—friend or foe.

BLACK

WHITE

**DIAGRAM 10a**
White's Bishop can capture the Black Rook or Pawn. It cannot capture the Black Knight because the White Pawn acts as an obstruction. It cannot capture the Black Queen, which is on a white square.

BLACK

WHITE

**DIAGRAM 10b**
White's Bishop has captured the Black Rook (see Diagram 10a).

## THE KNIGHT

Unlike the Queen, Rook, and Bishop, the Knight has a move of uniform length. It always moves two squares in the following manner: one square up or down or sideways and then one move diagonally still moving away from the square on which it started. Diagram 11a shows eight possible Knight moves.

BLACK

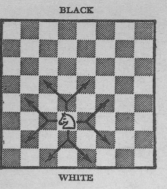

WHITE

DIAGRAM 11a
The arrows show eight
possible moves that can
be made by the Knight.

In Diagram 11b we eliminate the arrows and use crosses to indicate the possible moves that can be made by the Knight.

BLACK

WHITE

DIAGRAM 11b
The crosses mark the
eight squares to which
the Knight has a choice
of moving (see
Diagram 11a).

It is one of the interesting features of the Knight's move that he always changes the color of his square. If he starts out on a white square (as in Diagram 11b) he moves to a black square. If he starts on a black square, he ends up on a white square.

BLACK

WHITE

DIAGRAM 11c
This is one of the eight possible moves that the Knight could have made in Diagrams 11a and 11b. Note that the Knight has moved from a white square to a black square.

Another interesting aspect of the Knight is that it is the only piece on the chessboard that can leap over other chessmen, friendly or hostile.

Note that in capturing, however, the Knight can capture only on the end-square of its move.

BLACK

WHITE

DIAGRAM 12a
White's Knight can capture *any* one of the Black Pawns. He simply leaps over the other chessmen to make the capture.

**BLACK**

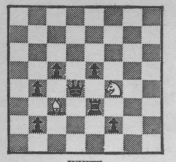

**WHITE**

DIAGRAM 12b
White's Knight has
captured one of the
Black Pawns (see
Diagram 12a).

## THE PAWN

The Pawn, though the least valuable of the chessmen, has
many interesting and useful qualities.

To begin with, the Pawn can move in only one direction—
straight ahead. If a Pawn's advance leaves it dangerously exposed to attack, it cannot retreat; it must be protected in one
fashion or another.

In most cases, the Pawn's forward move consists of advancing one square. (There is one exception to this rule, which
we shall consider a little later on.)

**BLACK**

**WHITE**

DIAGRAM 13a
White Pawns move
toward the Black side.
Black Pawns move
toward the White side.

The advance of the Pawns would lead to the position shown in Diagram 13b.

**BLACK**

DIAGRAM 13b
Each Pawn has advanced one square (see Diagram 13a).

**WHITE**

There is one important exception to the rule for advancing a Pawn one square.

Whenever a Pawn is still on its original square on the second rank (see Diagram 2), it has the option of advancing one square or two. This option can be exercised at *any time* in the game, so long as the Pawn in question has not been moved.

Let's imagine, for example, that in the situation of Diagram 2 White chooses to advance his King Pawn two squares, and that Black in turn decides to advance his Queen Bishop Pawn one square. This would give us the position of Diagram 14.

**BLACK**

DIAGRAM 14
White has advanced his King Pawn two squares. Black has advanced his Queen Bishop Pawn only one square.

**WHITE**

The Pawn is the only chessman which does not capture the same way it moves.

As we know, the Pawn moves by going forward one square (with the option of advancing two squares the first time it moves). When it comes to capturing, however, it can only remove hostile chessmen that are *one square diagonally forward of it.*

The important thing to remember is that the Pawn cannot capture any chessman *directly* in front of it. In that case, the hostile man merely blocks the Pawn's further progress.

**BLACK**

**WHITE**

DIAGRAM 15a
White's King Knight Pawn can capture the Black Bishop *or* the Black Knight. Black's Queen Knight Pawn can capture the White Rook *or* the White Queen. Neither of the King Pawns can capture the other. Each King Pawn blocks the other's advance.

To get a picture of the mechanics of Pawn capture, we can turn to Diagram 15b.

**BLACK**

**WHITE**

DIAGRAM 15b
White's King Knight Pawn has captured the Black Knight. Black's Queen Knight Pawn has captured the White Queen (see Diagram 15a).

### CHECK AND CHECKMATE

It was stated earlier—without explanation—that the King is the most important piece in chess. We are now ready to have the explanation.

A game of chess is won by *subjecting the hostile King to an attack from which he cannot escape.* This is known as "checkmate." In checkmate situations the King is not captured; it is enough to establish that the King cannot be saved.

Very often when a player sees that checkmate cannot be avoided, he "resigns." This means that he officially concedes defeat. However, if he refuses to admit defeat, then the player who has the advantage can win only by executing a checkmate.

When a King is under attack, we say he is in "check." Diagram 16a shows such a situation.

BLACK

WHITE

DIAGRAM 16a
Black's King is attacked by White's Queen. We say that Black's King is in check, or that the White Queen is checking the Black King.

When a player's King is in check, he must get him out of check at once. If he cannot get his King out of check, then he is checkmated. The game is over—he has lost.

There are three possible ways to get a King out of check. One way is to move the King to some square that is not in the capturing range of any hostile chessman.

Another way is to capture the chessman that is giving check.

The remaining way is "interposition"—placing one of your chessmen on the line of attack in order to screen your King from check.

Let's take another look at Diagram 16a. It might seem at

BLACK

WHITE

DIAGRAM 16b
Black has moved his
King out of check by
making a horizontal
move with his King
(see Diagram 16a).

first sight that Black has a choice of three King moves to get
out of check. But actually he has only a single move for the
purpose.

For example, he cannot make a vertical move with his
King, as this would bring him within the capturing range of
White's King.

Nor can Black make a diagonal move with his King, as
this would also bring him within the capturing range of
White's King—and would still leave him exposed to check by
White's Queen.

All that is left for Black, then, is a horizontal move of his
King. This gives us the situation of Diagram 16b.

Suppose that Black selects one of the other methods of
getting out of check—capturing the chessman that is giving
check. Then we have the position of Diagram 16c.

BLACK

WHITE

DIAGRAM 16c
Black has gotten out of
check by capturing the
White Queen with his
Rook (see Diagram
16a).

There is still one other way of getting out of check that we have to consider, and that is interposing a chessman on the line of attack. How would you do this in the position of Diagram 16a?

**BLACK**

**WHITE**

DIAGRAM 16d
Black has gotten out of check by interposing his Bishop (see Diagram 16a).

But suppose that all these methods of getting out of check are not available? Then we have a checkmate position.

**BLACK**

**WHITE**

DIAGRAM 17
Black is checkmated. Note that Black's King is on the last rank, where he is deprived of a retreat.

White's Queen is giving check. Black's King cannot capture the Queen, for this would bring him inside the capturing range of White's King. Any other move of the Black King would similarly leave him inside the capturing range of White's Queen or King, or both. And interposition is impossible.

If we substitute a White Rook for the White Queen in Diagram 17, then we now no longer have a checkmate position. For in that case Black can get out of check by playing his King to the right or left.

In Diagram 18, however, we have a situation in which either a Queen or a Rook can deliver checkmate.

BLACK

DIAGRAM 18
Black is checkmated. If we substitute a White Rook for the White Queen, Black is still checkmated.

WHITE

Once more we apply the same tests for checkmate: Black cannot capture the checking unit; he cannot interpose; he cannot move outside the capturing range of the White pieces.

It is impossible to force checkmate with a single Bishop or Knight, or even with two Knights; but it can be done with two Bishops, and Diagram 19 shows a typical position of this kind.

BLACK

DIAGRAM 19
Black is checkmated. This type of checkmate is feasible only when the King has been driven into a corner.

WHITE

It is also possible to checkmate with a Bishop and Knight, as we see in Diagram 20.

BLACK

WHITE

**DIAGRAM 20**
Black is checkmated. In this case too, the King has to be driven into a corner.

There are several points that are derived from what we have learned about check and checkmate. The most important of these is that you can never make a move that exposes your King to check. If you do, you must take back the move.

Captures are optional in chess, but if a capture would expose your King to check, you cannot make that capture. On the other hand, if a capture is the only way to get your King out of check, then that capture becomes compulsory.

## DISCOVERED CHECK AND DOUBLE CHECK

We use the term "discovered" in the sense of "uncovered." We mean a check that comes into existence when a chessman moves off a line and thereby uncovers a check by another man *which does not move.* Diagram 21a shows a situation where a discovered check is possible.

Diagram 21b illustrates an interesting point about many discovered checks. The piece that moves away—in this case the Bishop—can often attack a valuable man in the process.

In this case, for example, the Bishop attacks Black's Queen. Black would like to save his Queen, but he has no choice—he has to get his King out of check. He can do this in various

**BLACK**

**WHITE**

**DIAGRAM 21a**
White can give a
discovered check by
moving his Bishop.

**BLACK**

**WHITE**

**DIAGRAM 21b**
By moving his Bishop,
White gives a
discovered check with
his Rook (see
Diagram 21a).

ways—by moving his King, or by interposing his Knight or his Queen. But no matter what he does, he has to lose his valuable Queen, because of the discovered check.

A special form of the discovered check, known as a "double check," occurs when the chessman that is uncovering the check also gives check. Returning to the position of Diagram 21a, can you see what Bishop move will enable White to give a double check?

Note the power of a double check, as revealed in Diagram 21c. Black cannot capture the Rook as he will still be in check from the Bishop. He cannot capture the Bishop as he will still be in check from the Rook. Interposition is similarly ruled out.

In fact, we have to conclude that the only reply to a double

DIAGRAM 21c
White is giving double
check with his Rook
and Bishop (see
Diagram 21a).

check is to move the King. Where this is not possible, double
check turns into immediate checkmate.

## CASTLING

Now that we have seen some of the dangers to which the
all-important King is exposed, we can appreciate a very
special move known as "castling." This process gets the King
away from the center of the board, which is generally the
most dangerous area for him.

Though castling counts as a single move, it actually involves
two moves: one with the King, and one with a Rook.

There are two kinds of castling: King-side castling, with
the King Rook; and Queen-side castling, with the Queen
Rook.

DIAGRAM 22a
Before King-side
castling (with the
King Rook).

To castle King-side, White moves his King two squares in the direction of his King Rook, and then places the Rook on the other side of his King. Black castles in the same way. See Diagram 22b.

DIAGRAM 22b
After King-side castling
(see Diagram 22a).

Castling Queen-side leads to a slightly different position, as there are three squares between the King and the Queen Rook (instead of a gap of two squares as on the King-side).

DIAGRAM 23a
Before Queen-side
castling (with the
Queen Rook).

To castle Queen-side, you move the King two squares in the direction of the Queen Rook, and then place the Queen

Rook on the other side of the King. This gives us the position of Diagram 23b.

BLACK

WHITE

DIAGRAM 23b
After Queen-side castling (see Diagram 23a).

There are a number of essential rules which govern the possibility of castling.

Two conditions make it impossible to castle altogether. If the King has moved, then castling is permanently ruled out.

BLACK

WHITE

DIAGRAM 24
White has moved his King. Therefore he cannot castle.

The other condition that makes castling permanently impossible is a Rook move. If the King Rook has moved, a player cannot castle King-side. However, this does not rule out his castling Queen-side, if all other necessary conditions are fulfilled.

**BLACK**

**WHITE**

DIAGRAM 25
White cannot castle
King-side because his
King Rook has been
moved. However, he
can castle Queen-side
with his unmoved
Queen Rook.

Sometimes castling is temporarily impossible for reasons that can be remedied. Once these conditions disappear, castling again becomes possible.

There are four such temporary conditions, and we shall now give examples of them.

The first temporary condition is that the squares between the King and Rook are not empty.

**BLACK**

**WHITE**

DIAGRAM 26
Black cannot castle
Queen-side because his
Queen Knight is still on
its original square.
However, King-side
castling is feasible.
White can castle
Queen-side, but not
King-side.

Castling is impossible if the King has to pass over a square controlled by the enemy.

**DIAGRAM 27**
Black cannot castle King-side because White's Bishop controls the black square over which the Black King must pass. White cannot castle Queen-side because Black's Rook controls the white square over which the White King must pass.

Castling is impossible if the King will wind up on a square commanded by the enemy.

**DIAGRAM 28**
Black cannot castle King-side because White's Bishop commands the white square on which the King would land. White cannot castle Queen-side because Black's Queen controls the black square on which the White King would land.

Castling is impossible when the King is in check.

BLACK

WHITE

DIAGRAM 29
White cannot castle
because his King is in
check. But he can
capture Black's Knight
with his Bishop; then,
after Black recaptures
with his Pawn, White
can castle.

We must emphasize once more that the castling difficulties illustrated in Diagrams 26-29 do not permanently deprive the King of the castling privilege. On the other hand, Diagrams 24-25 illustrate situations where castling (on one side or both) is permanently impossible.

## MORE POWERS OF THE PAWN

While the Pawn is the weakest of the chessmen, it should not be despised; it does have one power which gives it enormous potential strength. This is the possibility of Pawn promotion, or "queening."

When a player advances a Pawn to the last square in a file, he can replace the Pawn with a new Queen, Rook, Bishop, or Knight. With very few exceptions, he selects a new Queen, as this is the most powerful piece on the board. Hence the term, "queening."

To obtain a new Queen in this way virtually assures victory, as one's opponent is reduced to helplessness. Diagram 30a is a startling example of this tremendously enhanced power.

**DIAGRAM 30a**
(White to play)
BEFORE QUEENING
White is "only" a Pawn ahead. He advances his Queen Rook Pawn (now on the seventh rank) to the last rank, and replaces it with a new Queen. See Diagram 30b.

**DIAGRAM 30b**
(Black is checkmated)
AFTER QUEENING
White has just obtained a new Queen by Pawn promotion. He is giving check. In fact, Black is checkmated!

In order to avoid confusion on the subject of Pawn promotion, we have to remember that White Pawns are promoted on White's last rank, while Black Pawns—*moving in the opposite direction*—are promoted on Black's last rank. This is made clear in Diagrams 31a and 31b.

Another curious power of the Pawn is its ability to capture *en passant* (in passing). The rules for this type of capture must be studied with great care.

To begin with, only Pawns can capture *en passant,* and only Pawns can be captured *en passant.*

## DIAGRAM 31
**BEFORE QUEENING**
White advances his
Pawn to his last rank
and replaces the Pawn
with a new Queen.
Black then advances
his Pawn to *his* last
rank and replaces the
Pawn with a new
Queen. (See Diagram
32).

## DIAGRAM 32
**AFTER QUEENING**
Both sides have
promoted their Pawns
to new Queens. (See
Diagram 31).

The Pawn that is going to be captured must be on its
original rank—its second rank.

The Pawn that captures must be on its fifth rank.

The two Pawns must be on adjoining files.

Diagram 33a shows a typical situation.

If Black should advance his Queen Pawn two squares,
White in reply can capture the Black Pawn *as if it had advanced only one square*. Diagram 33b shows the position
before the capture is made.

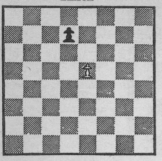

**BLACK**

**WHITE**

**DIAGRAM 33a**
(Black to play)
Note the basic features
of an *en passant*
capture: the Pawns are
on adjoining files; one
Pawn is on its fifth
rank, the other on its
second rank. Black now
advances his Pawn two
squares (see Diagram
33b).

**BLACK**

**WHITE**

**DIAGRAM 33b**
(White to play)
Black has just
advanced his Queen
Pawn two squares.
White can now capture
the Black Pawn. See
Diagram 33c for the
resulting position.

Diagram 33c shows the position that results from White's
*en passant* capture.

There are several further points to be noticed about *en
passant* capture. The capture is optional. However, if you
don't exercise the option to capture at the very first opportunity, you lose your chance for good.

The only times that *en passant* captures involve an element
of compulsion is when the safety of the King is involved. For
example, if an *en passant* capture would expose your King

**BLACK**

**WHITE**

DIAGRAM 33c
White has captured
*en passant* (see
Diagram 33b).

to attack, then the capture cannot be made. On the other
hand, if an *en passant* capture is the only way to get out of
check, then you must make the capture.

## THE CHESS NOTATION

It is of the utmost importance to be able to describe and
record moves. This enables you to write down the moves of
your games. What is perhaps even more important, it enables
you to read chess books for purposes of study and enjoyment.

The system for recording moves is called "chess notation."
This involves giving each piece a name and each square a
name. The best way to see how this is done is to re-examine
the starting position.

**BLACK**

**WHITE**

DIAGRAM 34
The starting position.

A quick review of the names of the pieces, Pawns, and files would be timely at this point. Starting at the extreme left, the pieces are named as follows:

| NAME | ABBREVIATION |
|------|-------------|
| Queen Rook | QR |
| Queen Knight | QN |
| Queen Bishop | QB |
| Queen | Q |
| King | K |
| King Bishop | KB |
| King Knight | KN |
| King Rook | KR |

The Pawns are named for the files on which they are placed, which in turn get their names from the opening placement of the chessmen. For example, the Queen Rook file and Queen Rook Pawn get their names from the Queen Rook's original position. This applies to Black chessmen as well as White chessmen.

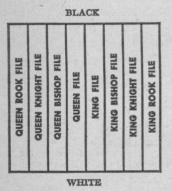

DIAGRAM 35
The names of the files.

Thus we see that each file has one name and only one name. The King file has the same name for Black as for White.

When we come to the ranks the situation is somewhat different. Each rank has a White name and a Black name.

The back rank on which White's pieces are placed at the beginning of the game is White's first rank. The next rank, on which his Pawns are placed, is White's second rank. The rank in front of that one is his third rank, and so on up to the last rank, which is White's eighth rank.

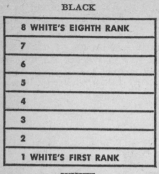

DIAGRAM 36a
The names of the ranks from White's side of the board.

Black employs the same system. The back rank on which he places his pieces at the beginning of the game is *his* first rank (White's eighth rank). The rank on which his Pawns go is his second rank (White's seventh rank). The rank immediately in front of Black's Pawns is Black's third rank (White's sixth rank). Black's fourth rank is White's fifth rank, and so on.

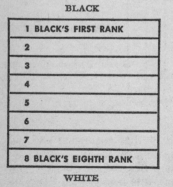

DIAGRAM 36b
The names of the ranks from Black's side of the board.

Now that we have identified the files and ranks, we are ready for our conclusion: *the name of any square on the chessboard is derived from the file and rank on which it stands.*

This proposition has a corollary, namely that each square has two names—one depending on White's method of counting the ranks, and one depending on Black's method of counting the ranks.

When we are dealing with a White move, we use the White system for naming the ranks. When we are dealing with a Black move, we use the Black system for naming the ranks.

Let's see how this works out in the naming of an individual square.

BLACK

WHITE

DIAGRAM 37
The square marked
with a cross is White's
King 4 square or
Black's King 5 square.

In Diagram 37 the heavy lines mark off the King file and a rank known as White's fourth rank or Black's fifth rank. Consequently the square marked with a cross is White's King 4 square, or Black's King 5 square.

Diagram 38 shows how this system is applied to the whole board.

If we want to record the two-square advance of White's King Pawn, we can write, "Pawn to King 4." If in reply Black advances his Queen Bishop Pawn one square, we can write, ". . . Pawn to Queen Bishop 3." (When the moves are not arranged in vertical columns, it is a good idea to precede the Black moves with several dots, in order to distinguish them from White moves.) See Diagram 14 for the resulting position.

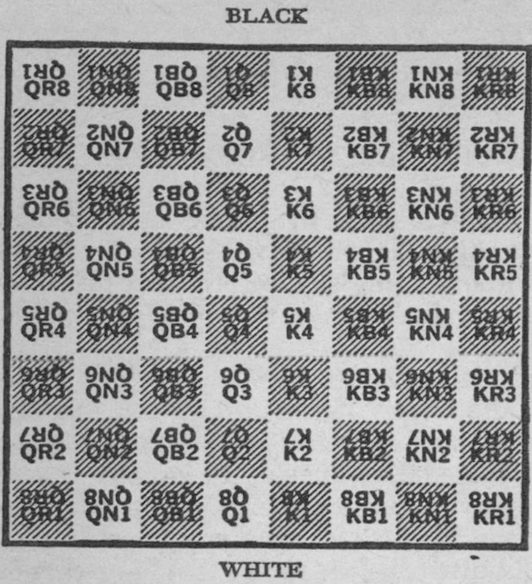

BLACK

DIAGRAM 38
The full chessboard, showing the double name of each square, from White's side of the board, and from Black's.

WHITE

You will have noted that in Diagram 38 we use abbreviations for the names of the squares, partly because there is no room for the full names, partly because it is convenient and time-saving to use abbreviations. It is quite clear that "K4" stands for "King 4," and that "KN7" stands for "King Knight 7."

Following the same line of reasoning, we abbreviate moves as well, substituting "P—K4" for "Pawn to King 4" and ". . . P—QB3" for ". . . Pawn to Queen Bishop 3."

In addition we have a number of abbreviations and symbols for several other standard items. Here they are:

| | |
|---|---|
| moves to | — |
| captures | x |
| check | ch |
| discovered check | dis ch |
| double check | dbl ch |
| *en passant* | e.p. |
| (in passing) | |
| good move | ! |
| bad move | ? |
| very good move | !! |

| very bad move | ?? |
| from, at | / |
| promotes to a Queen | /Q |

## RELATIVE VALUES OF THE CHESSMEN

Many—if not most—games are won by getting an advantage in material. This means either that you have captured material from your opponent without losing any, or else that the units you captured were more valuable than the units you lost in return.

To be ahead in material means that you have more force at your disposal than the enemy has. You can use this advantage in force for winning purposes—to checkmate your opponent, to win more material, to queen a Pawn, etc.

It is therefore necessary to place some standard valuation on each type of chessman to know whether any possible capture is desirable or disadvantageous. Since the King cannot be captured, we have no valuation for him. As for the other men, they have been given the following values:

| Queen | 9 points |
| Rook | 5 points |
| Bishop | 3 points |
| Knight | 3 points |
| Pawn | 1 point |

One of the things that is clear from this table is that a Bishop and Knight are equal in value, so that if one player captures a Bishop and the other captures a Knight, the material relationship remains the same.

It is advantageous to win a Rook in return for losing a Bishop or Knight; this is known as "winning the Exchange."

It is disadvantageous to lose a Rook in return for winning a Bishop or Knight; this is known as "losing the Exchange."

A Queen is worth much more than a Rook, and is superior to a Rook and Knight—or Rook and Bishop.

While it is generally advantageous to win material, there are times when it can be given away, in order to achieve some worthwhile objective—such as checkmate or the gain of more material. However, such "sacrifices" and "combinations" have to be calculated with great accuracy. A faulty calculation will generally lead to loss of the game.

### BRIEF GAMES

In order to familiarize you with the notation, we shall study some short games which illustrate common errors of beginners. Set up the pieces in the position of Diagram 34.

|   | WHITE | BLACK |
|---|-------|-------|
| 1 | P–KB3? | P–K4 |
| 2 | P–KN4?? | Q–R5 mate |

**BLACK**

**WHITE**

DIAGRAM 39
(White is checkmated)
The shortest possible game.

White cannot capture the Black Queen; he cannot move his King out of check; he cannot interpose. Therefore he is checkmated.

Both of his Pawn moves opened up the approaches to his King. You see, then, that from the very first move you must carefully guard your King against attack.

Set up the pieces again in the opening position.

|   | WHITE | BLACK |
|---|-------|-------|
| 1 | P–K4 | P–K4 |
| 2 | B–B4 | B–B4 |
| 3 | Q–R5 | . . . . |

White threatens 4 QxBP mate and also 4 QxKPch. Black sees the minor threat but not the major threat. Incidentally, he can meet both threats comfortably with 3 . . . Q–K2 or 3 . . . Q–B3.

|   |   |   |
|---|---|---|
| 3 | . . . . | N–QB3?? |

This guards the King Pawn but allows White to mate on the move.

4   QxBP mate

BLACK

WHITE

DIAGRAM 40
(Black is checkmated)
Black's King cannot capture the White Queen because she is protected by White's Bishop at Queen Bishop 4.

## DRAWN GAMES

So far we have been talking only about games that end in victory for one player and in defeat for his opponent.

But there is still another possibility—neither player wins. Such a game is called a "draw." Let's explore the various reasons that cause a game to reach a dead end.

## PERPETUAL CHECK

As the name indicates, a draw by perpetual check comes about when one player is in a position to give a series of checks from which his opponent cannot escape. Obviously there will usually be some compelling reason to induce a player to seek a draw in this way. Consider Diagram 41a, in which we find that White is a piece down.

Strictly speaking, White is really at no disadvantage in material in Diagram 41a, as he has three Pawns for a Bishop. However, the Pawns can only display their power at a very advanced and simplified stage of the game. So, feeling un-

BLACK

WHITE

DIAGRAM 41a
(White to play)
White can force a draw
by perpetual check. He
starts with 1 Q—R6ch.

comfortable, White decides to force a draw by perpetual
check. This is how he does it (see Diagram 41a):

| WHITE | BLACK |
|-------|-------|
| 1  Q—R6ch | . . . . |

Black's reply is forced.

| 1  . . . . | K—N1 |

Now White checks again.

| 2  Q—N6ch | . . . . |

This gives us the position of Diagram 41b.

BLACK

WHITE

DIAGRAM 41b
(Black to play)
Black cannot escape
from the perpetual
check.

2   ....      K—R1

We are now back to the position of Diagram 41a. It is clear that White can keep checking back and forth with his Queen and that Black is limited to moving his King back and forth in reply. Consequently White is able to force a draw by perpetual check.

### STALEMATE

Stalemate positions are drawn. A stalemate comes about when the following conditions have been met:

1. The player who claims the stalemate is about to move.
2. His King is not in check.
3. He is limited to moves which would put his King in check.

If all three conditions are present, the player is stalemated and the game is a draw.

Note how this differs from checkmate. In the case of checkmate, a player is already *in check* and is unable to get out of check. Diagrams 42a and 42b illustrate the difference between stalemate and checkmate.

**BLACK**

**WHITE**

DIAGRAM 42a
(*White* to play)
This is a stalemate
position.

White is stalemated.

All three factors of stalemate are present. It is his turn to move; his King is not in check; he is limited to moves that will put his King in check.

Now note the difference in Diagram 42b.

DIAGRAM 42b
(*Black* to play)
This is not a stalemate
position.

Though we have the same position, White is not stalemated
because *it is not his turn to play!*

It is Black's move, and he takes advantage of the situation
to play 1 . . . Q–QN7 mate.


## OTHER DRAWING METHODS

These include the following:

1. The players can agree to call the game a draw.

2. In the unlikely event that 50 moves have been made
by each player without a capture or a Pawn move, either
player has the option of claiming a draw. This rule doubtless
started as a penalty on a player who has a great advantage in
material but lacks the skill to enforce checkmate.

3. If the same position is about to be brought about for
the third time, with the same player on the move in each
case, he can claim a draw before producing the threefold
repetition.

4. Many a draw results from the fact that a player's advantage in material in the final stage is insufficient to force
checkmate. A lone King cannot be checkmated by any of the
following:

    (a) King and Bishop against King.

    (b) King and Knight against King.

    (c) King and two Knights against King.

# 2

# CHECKMATE PATTERNS
# AND CHECKING ATTACKS

How does a beginner learn to be a good player? The customary way of presenting the subject is to start with the opening phase, go on to the middle game, and eventually to discuss the endgame. This is a logical sequence because it parallels the ordinary course of a game.

But I propose a quite different method. After studying many thousands of the games of average players, I found in almost all of them the same flaw: mechanical moves, made with little or no thought about a goal, an objective, a direct means to victory. Given this indecisive frame of mind, what can the beginner learn about the opening that will be meaningful and useful to him?

Consequently I will first show you how games are won—how the opposing King is checkmated. I will select examples that are particularly impressive, so that the lesson will be vivid and remain fixed in the reader's mind when he plays his own games.

Our guiding thought, then, is that the first qualification for being a good player is to know how to checkmate your opponent. To learn how to checkmate is not easy, because checkmate positions can take so many varied forms.

But we can make the job easier by examining checkmate patterns—skeleton outlines of the most common kinds of checkmates. This will help us to understand—and use—these fundamental patterns in our own games.

## QUEEN AND PAWN CHECKMATE PATTERNS

We begin with patterns in which a Pawn assists the Queen to deliver checkmate.

**DIAGRAM 43a**
(White to play)
White's Queen and
King Bishop Pawn will
co-operate to
checkmate on King
Knight 7.

White plays 1 Q—N7 mate, giving us the position of
Diagram 43b.

**DIAGRAM 43b**
(Black is checkmated)
Black's King has no
escape, as White's
Queen is guarded by
his Pawn at King
Bishop 6.

Note that we can get the same effect with a White Queen
on King Bishop 6 and a White Pawn at King Rook 6. It is
still possible to play 1 Q—N7 mate.

For a more complicated example of the same theme we turn
to Diagram 44a.

BLACK

WHITE

DIAGRAM 44a
(White to play)
How will White's
Queen and his King
Bishop Pawn
co-operate to force
checkmate?

After what we have just learned, we find that White's move is quite obvious.

WHITE      BLACK
1   Q–R6      . . . .

With the help of his far advanced Pawn, White threatens 2 Q–N7 mate. However, in this case Black has a defense.

1 . . . .      R–KN1

Black guards his King against the threatened Q–N7 mate.

It now seems that White has reached a dead end. But this is not so; he continues the attack by putting Black's defensive Rook out of commission.

2   R–Q8!      . . . .

Beautiful play: White offers a Rook in order to bring about checkmate.

BLACK

WHITE

DIAGRAM 44b
(Black to play)
Black must not play 2
. . . RxR?? as this
allows 3 Q–N7 mate.

We see after all that White's daring Rook is safe from capture.

But more is involved: White's Rook at Queen 8 "pins" Black's defensive Rook. That is to say, Black's Rook at King Knight 1 cannot move off the rank because such a move would expose the Black King to check. Since this Black Rook cannot move, *White is threatening 3 Q–N7 mate.* (There is also a secondary threat of 3 RxRch, KxR; 4 Q–N7 mate, as in Diagram 43b.)

2 . . . . R/K5–K1

This is the best Black can do. He "unpins" his Rook at King Knight 1 and thus prevents Q–N7 mate–but only for a moment.

3 RxR Resigns

Black concedes defeat because he is helpless against the coming 4 Q–N7 mate.

Of course, if Black plays 3 . . . RxR, White replies 4 Q–N7 mate.

Now let's turn to a similar mating pattern involving the co-operation of Queen and Pawn.

BLACK

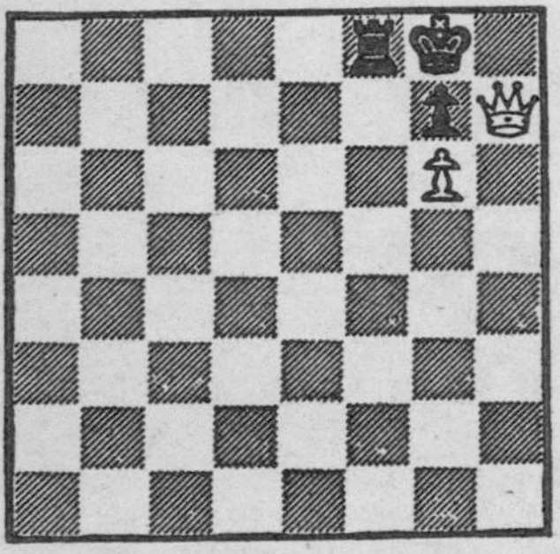

WHITE

DIAGRAM 45
(Black is checkmated)
White's Queen, assisted by his King Knight Pawn, gives checkmate on King Rook 7.

White has just played Q–KR7 mate. This is made possible by the fact that his King Knight Pawn protects his Queen.

BLACK

DIAGRAM 46a
(Black to play)
Black can force mate
in three moves.

WHITE

The simplest and quickest way for Black to win is to make use of the pattern shown in Diagram 45.

| WHITE | BLACK |
|---|---|
| 1 . . . . | R—R8ch!! |

This "sacrifice" comes as a great surprise—if you do not know the pattern.

| 2 | KxR | Q—R3ch |
| 3 | K—N1 | Q—R7 mate |

See Diagram 46b.

BLACK

DIAGRAM 46b
(White is checkmated)
Black's Queen, assisted
by his King Knight
Pawn, gives checkmate
at King Rook 7.

WHITE

And in Diagram 47a we have another situation where our knowledge of the mating pattern in Diagram 45 pays off handsomely.

BLACK

WHITE

DIAGRAM 47a
(Black to play)
Black can force
checkmate in two
moves.

Black can play 1 . . . QxQNP with two Pawns ahead and a win which will take some time. Instead, he can win at once with:

> WHITE          BLACK
> 1 . . . .      RxPch!

An apparently senseless sacrifice.

> 2  PxR        Q—R7 mate

See Diagram 47b.

BLACK

WHITE

DIAGRAM 47b
(White is checkmated)
Black's Queen, assisted
by his King Knight
Pawn, gives checkmate
at King Rook 7. (Note
the basic pattern of
Diagram 45.)

## QUEEN AND BISHOP CHECKMATE PATTERNS

Here we advance to more interesting patterns, as the Bishop can operate from a much greater distance than the Pawn. To start in the simplest manner, let's replace the White Pawn of Diagram 43a with a Bishop.

BLACK

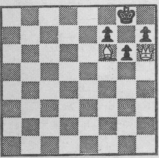

WHITE

DIAGRAM 48
(White to play)
White plays 1 Q—N7 mate. His Queen is protected by his Bishop.

This pattern can be varied in all sorts of ways. For example, the mate can be accomplished by a White Queen on King Bishop 6 backed up by a White Bishop on Queen Knight 2. (In that case, White can give mate on King Rook 8 as well as on King Knight 7.)

Also, there are times—depending on the angle of approach —when the Queen can mate on the target squares by means of a vertical or horizontal move. There are also situations in which a Rook can take the place of the Queen to force checkmate.

Now for some examples of this pattern: (see Diagram 49a). This position arose in a game in which the great Tarrasch played the Black pieces against a consulting team of amateurs. Tarrasch saw that his immediate threat of mate could be parried by the White Queen, to be sure. But he also realized that White's Queen had a second defensive task: to

BLACK

WHITE

DIAGRAM 49a
Black cannot play 1
. . . QxNP mate
because White's Queen
guards the threat. How
then should Black
proceed?

defend the White Rook. He therefore forced mate in this
fashion:

| WHITE | BLACK |
|-------|-------|
| 1 . . . . | RxRch |
| 2 QxR | . . . . |

White has no choice. But now that his Queen has disappeared from the second rank, Black can force mate.

     2 . . . .      QxNP mate

BLACK

WHITE

DIAGRAM 49b
(White is checkmated)
Black's Queen is
protected by his
Bishop.

The pattern of Diagram 48 turns up perfectly in Diagram
50a—if you can make a quick mental adjustment for an ap-
parent difference.

BLACK

WHITE

DIAGRAM 50a
(White to play)
White cannot play 1
QxBP mate because
Black replies 1 . . . ?
(See Solution A on
p. 137.)

White's witty first move certainly shows that he is familiar
with the pattern of Diagram 48, for he plays:

WHITE          BLACK
1   R–N8ch!    . . . .

This offer of a Rook seems to make no sense—but there is
method in his madness. Note that White's Queen and Bishop
are poised on the same diagonal for the mate that follows.

1 . . . .          KxR

Forced.

2   Q–N7 mate

BLACK

WHITE

DIAGRAM 50b
(Black is checkmated)
Compare this situation
with Diagram 48.

Note that Black's Queen was hopelessly out of play and incapable of doing anything for the defense. This uselessness of the defender's Queen is often a key factor in the success of an attack.

We mentioned earlier that a Rook can sometimes replace the Queen in a mating attack which also utilizes a Bishop. Diagram 51a illustrates such an attack.

BLACK

WHITE

DIAGRAM 51a
(White to play)
White would like to play 1 Q–R5ch in order to answer 1 . . . K–N1? with 2 Q–R8 mate. But Black reacts to 1 Q–R5ch with 1 . . . ? (See Solution B on p. 137.)

While White cannot use his Queen for a mating attack, his Rook on the third rank is fortunately available for the purpose. So White has his mating attack after all:

| WHITE | BLACK |
|-------|-------|
| 1  R–KR3ch | K–N1 |
| 2  R–R8 mate | |

BLACK

WHITE

DIAGRAM 51b
(Black is checkmated)
A typical mating pattern with Rook and Bishop.

In Diagram 52 we come across an amusing trap which expresses the clash between two markedly different personalities.

BLACK

WHITE

DIAGRAM 52
(White to play)
White can play 1
Q—Q7 or 1 Q—KB7.
Which is the right
move?

The position of Diagram 52 arose in a game played in a tournament at London in 1922. White was Milan Vidmar, a very strong player with a rather phlegmatic style; the player of the Black pieces was Savielly Tartakover, a lively, unconventional player with a habit of setting last-ditch traps in lost positions.

Of course, in one respect Diagram 52 presents no problem at all—White can win without any trouble by simply playing 1 BxR etc. But this would be too prosaic for White when he has a flashy Queen sacrifice with 1 Q—Q7 or 1 Q—B7. The point is that White is then threatening 2 QxR mate, and Black cannot play 1 . . . RxQ because of the reply 2 R—KR8 mate (our familiar mating pattern).

But White has to make up his mind—which Queen move should he play? Both are equally effective, it would seem; but this is the basis of Tartakover's sly trap. One of these moves wins—the other allows Black to draw! The proof:

| | WHITE | BLACK |
|---|---|---|
| 1 | Q—B7? | Q—Q8ch |
| 2 | K—R2 | Q—N6ch |
| 3 | K moves | Q—Q8ch |
| 4 | K—R2 | Q—N6ch |

And so forth. Black obviously has a draw by perpetual check.

The right move is therefore 1 Q—Q7! This threatens mate and also prevents 1 . . . Q—Q8ch, as White simply answers 2 QxQ. Actually, after 1 Q—Q7! Tartakover resigned, as he did not relish the continuation 1 . . . RxQ; 2 R—KR8 mate.

One of the most remarkable examples of this pattern in master play occurred in a game played at Warsaw in 1917 between the great Akiba Rubinstein and an obscure amateur named Belsitzmann. One of the most sensitive artists in the history of chess, Rubinstein was especially noted for the exquisite precision of his endgame play. He was equally at home, however, in combinations of extraordinary beauty and originality. We have a good proof of this in Diagram 53a, with Rubinstein handling the Black pieces.

BLACK

WHITE

DIAGRAM 53a
(Black to play)
Black's Knight at
Queen 5 is attacked.
How should Black
proceed?

The familiar mating pattern exists potentially in the position of Diagram 53a (co-operation of Black's Queen and his Bishop on the long diagonal). But of course as matters stand, Black cannot play 1 . . . Q—N7 mate as both White Knights prevent that possibility.

It seems, then, that Black has nothing better than to retreat his attacked Knight. But Rubinstein sees much farther into the position. He intends to make the mating pattern work; therefore he plays:

| WHITE | BLACK |
|-------|-------|
| 1 . . . . | P—KR4!! |
| 2 PxN | . . . . |

Why not? says White.

$$2 \;\dots\dots\qquad \text{P–R5}$$

Now we see what Rubinstein is getting at. He wants to open the King Rook file, bringing his King Rook into the attack. Thus he threatens, among other things, 3 . . . PxP; 4 BPxP, QxRP mate.

$$3 \quad \text{Q–K2}\qquad \dots\dots$$

White parries the threat by defending along the second rank. But now Rubinstein carries out his second and even finer threat.

$$3 \;\dots\dots\qquad \text{QxRPch!!}$$

Very beautiful play.

$$4 \quad \text{KxQ}\qquad \text{PxP dbl ch}$$

White cannot capture this Pawn, as it is guarded by Black's Bishop on Queen 3. This leaves White with only one reply.

$$5 \quad \text{K–N1}\qquad \text{R–R8 mate}$$

BLACK

DIAGRAM 53b
(White is checkmated)
Compare the mating situation in Diagram 51b.

WHITE

What is so impressive about Rubinstein's magnificent combination is that it shows us how the most sublime achievements of master play can be traced back to rather simple, *typical* patterns.

Diagram 54a teaches the same lesson in reverse. If we learned from Diagram 53a that the most dynamic combina-

tions can evolve from a fairly simple pattern, we find in
Diagram 54a that the most ludicrous consequences can flow
from disregard of the same simple pattern.

BLACK

WHITE

DIAGRAM 54a
(Black to play)
Black has a forced
mate!

The position of Diagram 54a turned up in a match played
in 1897 by two Russian masters, Schiffers (White) and
Tchigorin (Black).

Tchigorin was a man of enormous vitality and exuberance,
gifted with vivid imagination and the power to put his extraordinary ideas into moves that figuratively crackled and
stung. But this was definitely not his day. Early in the opening
he lost his Queen, which explains why he has only a Bishop
against White's Queen in the position of Diagram 54a.

But Schiffers, perhaps lulled by overconfidence, has also
played carelessly—so much so that Tchigorin has a forced
mate. The mate must depend in some way on our familiar
pattern, and here is how it proceeds:

| WHITE | BLACK |
|-------|-------|
| 1 . . . ; | R—R8ch!! |
| 2  NxR | B—R7ch!! |

Again White must capture.

|       |       |
|-------|-------|
| 3  KxB | R—R1ch |

Now we see what Black is getting at, for if White plays
4 K—N1 we get our familiar pattern with 4 . . . ? (See Solution C on p. 137.)

$$
\begin{array}{lll}
4 & K-N3 & N-B4ch \\
5 & K-B4 & \dots \\
\end{array}
$$

It doesn't matter whether White plays this or 5 K–N4.

5 .... R–R5 mate

See Diagram 54b.

BLACK

DIAGRAM 54b
(White is checkmated)
White's material
superiority is useless to
him.

WHITE

But this did not happen in the game! Instead, Tchigorin played the feeble 1 ... P–N3?? which should have lost for him. However, Schiffers continued his slovenly play and eventually the game ended in a draw.

We turn now to Diagram 55 for another basic pattern which calls for the co-operation of Queen and Bishop.

BLACK

DIAGRAM 55
(Black is checkmated)
Typical pattern for a
combined mating
attack by the Queen
and the King Bishop
(either by QxKRP mate
or by Q–KR7 mate).

WHITE

This pattern is admirably illustrated in Diagram 56a.

BLACK

DIAGRAM 56a
(White to play)
Note the formidable
power of White's two
powerful Bishops
trained on the
King-side (as in
Diagram 53a).

WHITE

White would like to play QxRP mate but this is impossible as long as Black's well-posted Knight guards the King-side. (Why isn't 1 QxRP mate feasible? See Solution D on p. 137.) This is where White's powerful two-Bishop barrage proves useful. He plays:

| WHITE | BLACK |
|-------|-------|
| 1  BxN! | . . . . |

White removes the valuable protective Knight.

| 1  . . . . | PxB |
|-----------|-----|
| 2  QxRP mate | |

BLACK

DIAGRAM 56b
(Black is checkmated)
Compare this situation
with Diagram 55.

WHITE

In Diagram 57a the kinship with our desired pattern is far from obvious. White's Bishop is on the right diagonal, but White's Queen is far from King Rook 7.

BLACK

WHITE

DIAGRAM 57a
(White to play)
White is inspired by
the pattern of
Diagram 55.

A lively sacrifice gives White the desired position:

| WHITE | BLACK |
|-------|-------|
| 1 R—R8ch! | KxR |

In the event of 1 . . . K—N2 White replies 2 P (See Solution E on p. 137.)

| 2 Q—R6ch | K—N1 |
| 3 Q—R7 mate | |

BLACK

WHITE

DIAGRAM 57b
(Black is checkmated)
White has achieved the
pattern of Diagram 55.

In Diagram 58a White has an easy win, but in chess the best win is the quickest win; and in this case the quickest win is achieved by applying the pattern of Diagram 55—with a slight adaptation.

BLACK

DIAGRAM 58a
(White to play)
Despite his deficit in material White has a quick win.

WHITE

White can win very quickly with 1 QxPch, K—B2; 2 RxPch, K—K1; 3 B—N6ch etc. But he has an even quicker way:

| WHITE | BLACK |
|---|---|
| 1  RxPch! | KxR |
| 2  QxP mate | |

BLACK

DIAGRAM 58b
(Black is checkmated)
The transposition of White's first and second moves led to a quicker win.

WHITE

## QUEEN AND KNIGHT CHECKMATE PATTERNS

Note one important difference between these patterns and those involving Queen and Bishop. The Bishop can take part in the mating process from a considerable distance. Not so the Knight; because of his short hop, he has to be on the fifth or sixth rank and right in the neighborhood of the attacked King.

Diagram 59 shows one of the most common patterns.

**BLACK**

**WHITE**

DIAGRAM 59
(Black is checkmated)
Compare this pattern
with Diagram 55.

Examples of the Diagram 59 pattern abound in practical play; for example:

**BLACK**

**WHITE**

DIAGRAM 60a
(White to play)
What move is called
for by the pattern of
Diagram 59?

With the pattern of Diagram 59 in mind, White forces mate in this manner:

| WHITE | BLACK |
|-------|-------|
| 1   N–N5 | . . . . |

White threatens 2 P (See Solution F on p. 137.)

| | |
|-------|-------|
| 1 . . . . | R–K1 |

Black creates an escape hatch for his King—but it will not save him in the end.

| | |
|-------|-------|
| 2   QxRPch | K–B1 |
| 3   QxBP mate | |

BLACK

WHITE

DIAGRAM 60b
(Black is checkmated)
Black has escaped from the pattern of Diagram 59, but he could not escape checkmate.

In Diagram 61a Black's King also has an escape hatch, but it proves useless.

BLACK

WHITE

DIAGRAM 61a
(White to play)
Show that 1 Q–B7ch leads to the win of Black's Queen.

While it is true that 1 Q–B7ch is a good move, White has an even quicker way to win:

| WHITE | BLACK |
|-------|-------|
| 1 QxPch | K–B1 |
| 2 Q–R8ch | K–K2 |
| 3 QxP mate | |

Returning to the caption of Diagram 61a, we note that 1 Q–B7ch, K–R1; 2 Q–R5 threatens 3 QxP mate and 3 N–B7ch winning the Queen. But of course the method given above is even better, as it *forces* checkmate.

BLACK

DIAGRAM 61b
(Black is checkmated)

WHITE

In our next example (Diagram 62a) White wins brilliantly because he is familiar with the pattern of Diagram 59.

BLACK

DIAGRAM 62a
(White to play)
Our first impression is that White has no more than a draw by perpetual check: 1 Q–R7ch, K–B1; 2 Q–B5ch, K–N1; 3 Q–R7ch, etc.

WHITE

White's problem in Diagram 62a is to nail down Black's King so that he cannot run away.

| WHITE | BLACK |
|-------|-------|
| 1   R—R8ch!! | KxR |

Of course Black cannot play 1 . . . BxR as his Bishop is pinned and must not expose the Black King to attack.

2   Q—R7 mate

**BLACK**

DIAGRAM 62b
(Black is checkmated)
White's Rook sacrifice
has prevented the flight
of the Black King.

**WHITE**

A related pattern calls for checkmate on King Rook 7 by the Queen, supported by a Knight at King Bishop 6 (Diagram 63).

**BLACK**

DIAGRAM 63
(Black is checkmated)
We can achieve the
same mate by
substituting a Rook for
the Queen.

**WHITE**

This Queen and Knight pattern is strikingly illustrated in Diagram 64a (executed by a Rook and Knight).

**DIAGRAM 64a**
(White to play)
It would be a mistake for White to play
1 N—B6ch, K—R1; 2 QxB because of the reply 2 . . . ? (See Solution G on p. 137.)

White wins by means of a spectacular Queen sacrifice:

| WHITE | BLACK |
|---|---|
| 1   QxBch! | PxQ |
| 2   N—B6ch | K—R1 |
| 3   R—R7 mate | |

**DIAGRAM 64b**
(Black is checkmated)
White's beautiful Queen sacrifice made this checkmate possible by removing Black's valuable protective Bishop from King Knight 3.

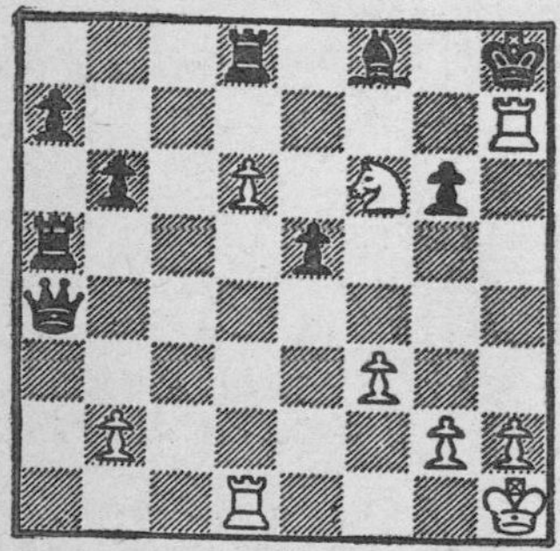

Sometimes the mating motif on King Rook 7 can be transformed into a checkmate on King Knight 8. Diagram 65a is a fine example.

BLACK

WHITE

DIAGRAM 65a
(Black to play)
Black would like to
play . . . Q—R5
(threatening the
pattern mate of
Diagram 63), but
White's Rook at King
Knight 4 seems to
block this plan.

Black wants to play 1 . . . Q—R5, but this seems impossible because of the reply 2 RxQ. But there is more to this position than meets the eye:

| WHITE | BLACK |
|---|---|
| 1 . . . . | Q—R5! |

If White replies 2 RxQ, Black hits back with 2 . . . R—N8 mate!

2 R—N2 . . . .

White defends himself against the threat of . . . QxRP mate.

2 . . . . QxRPch!!

The point of Black's combination.

3 RxQ R—N8 mate

BLACK

WHITE

DIAGRAM 65b
(White is checkmated)
Black has cleverly
deployed his forces for
a double mating attack
on King Rook 7 and
King Knight 8.

This splendid finish was brought off by Wilhelm Steinitz in a game played against an amateur named Reiner at Vienna in 1860. Steinitz was a very brilliant player in his youth, so much admired for the imaginative richness of his attacking ideas that he was nicknamed the "Austrian Morphy." This was praise indeed, for at that time the young American was the idol of the chess world.

One other Queen and Knight mating pattern remains to be noticed. Here the Queen mates on King Knight 7, supported by a Knight at King Bishop 5 or King Rook 5.

BLACK

DIAGRAM 66
(Black is checkmated)
Pattern for Queen and
Knight checkmate at
King Knight 7.

WHITE

The Queen will generally reach King Knight 7 from King Rook 6 or King Bishop 6.

BLACK

DIAGRAM 67a
(White to play)
White heads right for
the mate.

WHITE

The mating process may be a little hard to understand, as it doesn't start with a check. But anyone familiar with the pattern of Diagram 66 will have no trouble finding the right move:

| WHITE | BLACK |
|-------|-------|
| 1   Q—R6! | Resigns |

Black is helpless against the coming Q—N7 mate.

BLACK

WHITE

DIAGRAM 67b
(Black to play)
A perfect example of the mating pattern in Diagram 66. Black cannot prevent checkmate and must resign.

## ROOK ATTACKS ON THE SEVENTH RANK

A Rook placed on the seventh rank, deep in the heart of enemy territory, is admirably placed to wreak frightful damage. David Janowski, the famous Franco-Polish master, characterized this destructive quality admirably when he quipped that such a Rook was "a blind pig."

Diagram 68 shows a characteristic pattern with two Rooks doubled on the seventh rank.

BLACK

WHITE

DIAGRAM 68
(Black is checkmated)
Mating pattern for Rooks doubled on the seventh rank.

In Diagram 69a the Queen replaces one of the Rooks in exploiting the seventh rank.

BLACK

WHITE

DIAGRAM 69a
(White to play)
White forces mate in
four moves.

Black, who is attacking one of the White Rooks, expects his opponent to save the menaced Rook. White has other ideas, based on the position of this Rook on the seventh rank.

| WHITE | BLACK |
|---|---|
| 1  RxRPch! | KxR |

Of course, after 1 . . . K—N1 White plays 2 R/R7xPch and it is mate next move. (How? See Solution H on p. 137.)

|  | |
|---|---|
| 2  Q—R5ch | K—N1 |
| 3  Q—B7ch | . . . . |

The attack on the seventh rank.

|  | |
|---|---|
| 3  . . . . | K—R2 |
| 4  QxNP mate | |

BLACK

WHITE

DIAGRAM 69b
(Black is checkmated)
Triumph of the seventh
rank.

In the position of Diagram 70, Black's familiarity with the pattern of Diagram 68 allows him to win a Rook brilliantly.

BLACK

WHITE

DIAGRAM 70
(Black to play)
White's Rook at King
Knight 4 seems to offer
ample protection
against the
depredations of Black's
Rooks on the seventh
rank.

Black wins a Rook with **1 . . . QxR!** as White must not retake:

|   |         |                  |
|---|---------|------------------|
| 2 | PxQ     | RxPch            |
| 3 | K–R1    | R–R7ch           |
| 4 | K–N1    | R/QR7–KN7 mate   |

By way of transition to our next mating pattern (checkmate on the last rank), Diagrams 71a and 72a will deal with attacks on the seventh and eighth ranks.

BLACK

WHITE

DIAGRAM 71a
(Black to play)
In this apparently
colorless position, Black
has an amazing
winning move. Hint:
What distinction do
you draw from the
respective positions of
the two Queens? (See
Solution I on p. 137.)

In Diagram 71a neither side seems to have much scope for action. So Black's winning move comes as a solar plexus blow: 1 . . . R—K7!!

This threatens two seventh-rank mates: 2 . . . QxRP mate or 2 . . . Q—N7 mate.

Nor can Black answer 1 . . . R—K7!! with 2 RxR. For then Black winds up with 2 . . . QxR mate.

BLACK

WHITE

DIAGRAM 71b
(White is checkmated)
White parried the attack on his seventh rank, only to get mated on the last rank.

In Diagram 72a the decision is if anything even more abrupt.

BLACK

WHITE

DIAGRAM 72a
(White to play)
White's grip on the seventh rank makes it possible for him to break through in startling fashion.

In Diagram 72a White's Queen is attacked, and the natural reaction would be to place the Queen on a safe square, possibly by 1 Q—Q7. Instead, White wins in dashing style.

| WHITE | BLACK |
|-------|-------|
| 1 BxPch!! | PxB |

Or 1 . . . K–R1; 2 QxRch and mate next move.

     2 QxRch!!   . . . .

This is now feasible because both White Rooks are free to act on the seventh and eighth ranks.

| 2 . . . . | KxQ |
|----------------|-----|
| 3 R–B8ch | B–Q1 |
| 4 RxB mate | |

BLACK

WHITE

DIAGRAM 72b
(Black is checkmated)
An important
checkmate motif: one
Rook checks the Black
King, the other Rook
prevents his escape.

## MATE ON THE EIGHTH RANK

We conclude our mating patterns with attack on the last rank, which appeared earlier in Diagram 30b on page 33. Diagram 73 illustrates this pattern.

This attack is often successful in the heat of the battle, when players are so absorbed in their own plans that they overlook the danger facing them on their own first rank. A good example of this may be seen in Diagram 64a. Suppose the play had proceeded 1 N–B6ch, K–R1; 2 QxB?? when White threatens three apparently inescapable mates (3 QxP mate, 3 RxRP mate, or 3 Q–N8 mate). But in that case Black would have decided the game immediately with 2 . . . QxR mate—a back-rank mate.

DIAGRAM 73
(Black is checkmated)
Mate on the last rank.

In Diagram 74a White applies the pattern of Diagram 73 after an astonishing first move.

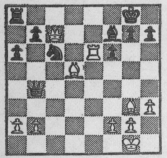

DIAGRAM 74a
(White to play)
If White plays 1
R—K4 (attacking
Black's Queen and
doubly attacking his
Bishop), Black saves
himself with 1 . . . ?
(See Solution J on p.
137.)

White's opening sacrifice is startling but effective:

| WHITE | BLACK |
|---|---|
| 1 R—K8ch! | . . . . |

Note that Black cannot capture 1 . . . BxR because his Bishop is pinned—it has the job of screening Black's King from attack by the White Bishop at Queen 5.

|   |        |       |
|---|--------|-------|
| 1 | . . . . | RxR   |
| 2 | QxBch  | K–R1  |
| 3 | QxRch  | Q–B1  |
| 4 | QxQ mate |     |

BLACK

DIAGRAM 74b
(Black is checkmated)
White's double attack
on the Black Bishop
prepared for an assault
on the last rank.

WHITE

With this example we conclude our study of checkmate patterns. Familiarity with these patterns should tell you a great deal about how to win by recognizing the favorable attacking opportunities.


## CHECKING ATTACKS

Since a check is an attack on the King, we must examine each check carefully for its incidental and often rewarding features. The point is this: *Suppose a check attacks another chessman in addition to the King.* The defender, preoccupied with getting his King out of danger, may find himself forced to lose the other attacked man.

This point is effectively brought out in Diagram 75a, in which White relies on a *double attack with check* to get out of his difficulties and at the same time score a decisive win of material.

BLACK

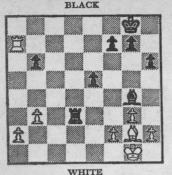

WHITE

DIAGRAM 75a
(White to play)
If it were Black's move
he could play 1 . . .
R—Q8ch; 2 B—B1,
B—R6 forcing mate on
the last rank. But it is
White's move, and he
can win with a
two-move checking
sequence.

Now that you have seen Black's threat, how would you meet it? Offense is the best defense, they say, and White agrees. So play proceeds:

| WHITE | BLACK |
|-------|-------|
| 1  R—R8ch | K—R2 |
| 2  B—K4ch | . . . . |

White gives check and at the same time attacks Black's Rook. Black has to get his King out of check and has no time to save his Rook.

BLACK

WHITE

DIAGRAM 75b
(Black to play)
White must win the
Black Rook. Black is
powerless against the
double attack.

Diagram 76a looks perfectly characterless, until we note that White's Queen pins the Black Queen. That is to say,

Black's Queen cannot move off the diagonal, as it screens Black's King from check.

BLACK

DIAGRAM 76a
(White to play)
How can White make
use of his pin on the
Black Queen?

WHITE

To exploit the pin, White combines the pin with a check.

| WHITE | BLACK |
|-------|-------|
| 1  R—Q1! | . . . . |

Still another pin. Of course Black cannot capture this Rook, as his Queen cannot move off the diagonal.

| | |
|-------|-------|
| 1  . . . . | QxQ |
| 2  RxRch! | . . . . |

Of course. The thoughtless alternative 2 PxQ??, RxRch leaves Black a Rook ahead.

BLACK

DIAGRAM 76b
(Black to play)
Black must move his
King out of check.
White continues 3
PxQ with a Rook to
the good.

WHITE

In Diagram 77a Black has recourse to one of the most popular (and most deadly) forms of attack: a Knight fork. This simultaneous attack on two or more chessmen becomes even more menacing when one of the Knight's targets is the opposing King.

**BLACK**

DIAGRAM 77a
(Black to play)
Black's Queen and
Knight are attacked.
Apparently he must
lose a piece.

**WHITE**

Many a player handling the Black pieces in this situation would give it up as hopeless. Yet Black need not lose any material; in fact, he wins some!

| WHITE | BLACK |
|-------|-------|
| 1 . . . . | QxR! |
| 2 NxQ | N–K7ch |

By removing White's Rook, Black made this Knight forking check possible.

**BLACK**

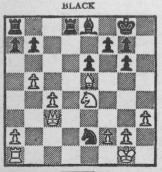

DIAGRAM 77b
(White to play)
In answer to the Knight
check, White must
move his King, giving
Black time to play 3
. . . NxQ.

**WHITE**

After Black has played 3 . . . NxQ and White has recaptured, Black is the Exchange ahead—he has a Rook for a Knight.

Diagram 78a is an interesting position which arose in a game between Perlis and Dus-Chotimirsky in the Carlsbad tournament of 1911. Perlis was a very promising young player who was killed two years later in a mountain-climbing accident. As for Dus-Chotimirsky, he was a young, brilliant, and somewhat eccentric master at this time. The story is told that during the course of his game with Emanuel Lasker (the World Champion) in the St. Petersburg tournament of 1909, Chotimirsky read a Japanese translation of *Thus Spake Zarathustra!* Legend has it that the World Champion was so incensed at the young man's studied insolence that he lost the game. Whatever the cause of his defeat, Lasker was singularly reticent about this encounter.

**BLACK**

**WHITE**

DIAGRAM 78a
(Black to play)
Black can win White's
Queen by a neat
tactical trick—a
combination of a pin
and Knight fork.

White seems safe enough—for example, after 1 . . . NxBch; 2 RxN, RxR; 3 QxR etc., Black has made no headway. Yet if Black is familiar with the pin and fork, he can smash up White's position.

| WHITE | BLACK |
|-------|-------|
| 1 . . . . | R—K8!! |

The proverbial bolt from the blue. As Black's Rook pins the White Queen, White has no choice.

|    2    QxR    |    NxBch    |

Now everything becomes clear. Black's Knight forks the White King and Queen. White's Knight Pawn is *pinned*, preventing him from playing 3 PxN.

So Black must choose between 3 RxN (allowing 3 . . .
QxQch in reply) or 3 K—B1 (allowing 3 . . . NxQ in reply).
In either case Black remains with a Queen for a Rook—an
easy win.

BLACK

DIAGRAM 78b
(White to play)
Black has cleverly
blended two powerful
attacking ideas—the
fork and the pin. His
Knight, which forks
White's King and
Queen, cannot be
captured by White's
pinned Knight Pawn.

WHITE

Another important attacking theme is discovered check,
discussed earlier in connection with Diagram 21a on p. 26.
Here is an impressive example from actual play:

BLACK

DIAGRAM 79
(White to play)
White wins by a deadly
discovered check,
namely 1 ? (See
Solution K on p. 137.)

WHITE

To conclude this chapter, we study an example of an X-ray
attack. This occurs when two pieces are attacked on the same
line—a rank, file, or diagonal. When the more valuable attacked piece moves off the line of attack, the second piece is
captured. As a rule the more valuable attacked piece is the
King—in other words, the X-ray attack is generally a check.

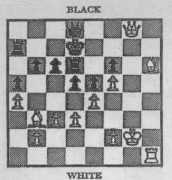

BLACK

WHITE

DIAGRAM 80a
(White to play)
White has a winning
X-ray attack if he plays
the right Queen check.
The question is, which
is the right check?

In Diagram 80a White has a winning material advantage—two Bishops and a Pawn for a Rook. Before we see how he achieves a quick win, it will be interesting to learn something about the players.

This game was played in a match in 1909 between José R. Capablanca (White) and Frank James Marshall (Black). Marshall was the United States Champion and a master of world fame. He was also an extraordinarily brilliant tactician, who relied more on inspiration than on the foresight and calculation which are supposed to be the hallmarks of a great chess master.

Capablanca, on the other hand, was virtually an unknown in the chess world. At the time the match was played, he was twenty years old, a junior at Columbia University, and had never played in an international tournament. Yet the earliest games of the match immediately revealed that he had a phenomenal natural facility for the game. In the grueling contest of 23 games with his far more seasoned opponent, the younger man won 8 games, lost only 1, and drew 14. On the strength of this single success he was at once catapulted into the front rank of great masters.

To return to Diagram 80a. The presence of Black's King and Rook on his second rank suggest the possibility of an X-ray check for White. But which check? In the event of 1 Q—B7ch or 1 Q—N7ch Black does not obligingly move his King (allowing 2 QxR). Instead, he plays 1 . . . Q—K2—which enables him to hold the position for the time being. The right way, therefore, is:

|  | WHITE | BLACK |
|---|---|---|
| 1 | Q—R7ch! | Q—K2 |

So far, so good, says Black.

|  |  |  |
|---|---|---|
| 2 | B—B8! | . . . . |

The winning move. To begin with, it enables White's Rook to protect the White Queen.

Secondly, Black's Queen is pinned and cannot capture the Bishop.

BLACK

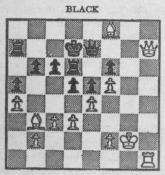

DIAGRAM 80b
(Black to play)
White's X-ray attack dooms Black's Rook at Queen Rook 2.

WHITE

Black is in a hopeless predicament. As his Queen is attacked, he has only one move:

|  |  |  |
|---|---|---|
| 2 | . . . . | QxQ |

But now White's X-ray attack achieves its purpose.

|  |  |  |
|---|---|---|
| 3 | RxQch | K—K1 |
| 4 | RxR | Resigns |

After 4 . . . KxB Black would be a piece and a Pawn down —a hopeless situation.

With this example we conclude our study of checkmate patterns and checking attacks. The checkmate patterns should be extremely helpful to you in finding objectives for decisive attacking methods; the checking attacks show you how to gain an overwhelming advantage in material which will lead to eventual victory.

Now we come to a new problem: How do we arrive at the kinds of positions in which we can make use of these winning patterns? This will be the subject matter of Chapter 3.

# 3
# THE BASIC PRINCIPLE
# OF OPENING PLAY

Weak players may differ in temperament and in experience, but they all have one characteristic in common: they play the opening badly. This becomes very clear if you ask them just what the opening is, or what is supposed to happen in the opening stage.

The opening is made up of the first ten moves or so—on both sides. It is the stage in which several pieces are brought out, placed on squares where they are ready to do battle with the enemy.

This process of getting out the pieces—or some pieces—is called "development." Watch a weak player's opening moves and you will see that the notion of developing his pieces is quite foreign to him. He is at a loss. He drifts. He makes an aimless move with a Pawn, and then moves it again on his next turn. He sticks to "safe" moves like P—KR3 and P—QR3.

He never asks himself, What am I achieving? What am I aiming for? How am I preventing my opponent from making headway?

You can never hope to win by playing aimless moves, by moving the same piece or Pawn repeatedly, by leaving your pieces on their home squares. You may win in this way through your opponent's blunders or oversights, but this is not a principle on which to depend. We must come to the conclusion that the right way to play the opening is to *develop your pieces*. This, in fact, is what the opening is all about. If you play the opening well, you will have good winning opportunities later on. If you play the opening badly, you will end up crushed by the weight of your resulting difficulties.

The concept of developing the pieces can be divided into a number of principles which often dovetail into one another. Most of these principles are negative—Don't do this and Don't do that.

What about positive, constructive examples? These are best taught by giving examples of actual play from the games of the great masters who have made development a fine art. The quickest way for you to gain an appreciation of the importance of development is to study games played by a great master against a feeble opponent. There you will see outlined, with the greatest possible clarity, the glaring contrast between powerful, purposeful development and feckless, thoughtless bumbling.

## ALWAYS PLAY 1 P—K4

This is a sound principle which will put you on the right track toward a good development. If you know in advance that this is to be your first move, you are saved from the indecision that results from trying to make a choice among the 20 theoretically possible first moves.

In addition, 1 P—K4 has other values. Most of the action in the opening centers about control of the center squares, because pieces posted in that area have more mobility (striking power) than in any other part of the board. Since the King Pawn is a center Pawn, its control of center squares is a great asset. Hostile pieces are debarred from occupying the squares controlled by this Pawn.

Still another asset of 1 P—K4 is that it opens up a diagonal for developing the King Bishop. (All this applies to Black as well.) A move like 1 P—KR3, for example, accomplishes nothing at all, as it fails to open up a line of development for any of the pieces; it contributes nothing to the problem of controlling the center; and it actually allows Black to take the initiative by playing 1 . . . P—K4.

Suppose a game starts out in this fashion:

| WHITE | BLACK |
|-------|-------|
| 1  P—K4 | . . . . |

White strives for quick development and control of the center.

| 1 . . . . | P—KR3? |

This achieves nothing.

| 2  P—Q4 | . . . . |

Now White has a magnificent Pawn center.

| 2 . . . . | P—R3? |

Another do-nothing move.

BLACK

WHITE

DIAGRAM 81
(White to play)
White's King and
Queen Pawns control
the center; his King
Bishop and Queen
Bishop can be
developed on splendid
diagonals. Black, on the
other hand, has done
nothing in the center
and nothing for his
development.

It would be a great mistake to consider Diagram 81 as a mere abstraction. Actually our appraisal of it can be projected far ahead. White will bring out his pieces rapidly and develop his pieces with formidable striking power. Black, thanks to his feeble opening moves, will never catch up in development; his position will remain uncomfortably constricted; he will be overwhelmed by White's pressure. It is no exaggeration to say that the position of Diagram 81—after two moves!—is lost for Black.

## AVOID EXCESSIVE PAWN MOVES

Here our reasoning is very similar. A player who keeps on making Pawn moves will be missing opportunities to develop his pieces and will soon find himself in serious trouble. Here is a sequence that illustrates the point:

| WHITE | BLACK |
|-------|-------|
| 1  P–K4 | P–K4 |
| 2  P–Q3? | . . . . |

A poor move. It blocks the diagonal of White's King Bishop, which has very little scope now.

                    2  . . . .        N–KB3

Black develops a piece.

                    3  P–KR3?        . . . .

Not knowing what to do, White makes an aimless Pawn move.

3 ....      B—B4

Black develops another piece.

4 P—R3?      ....

White is still floundering.

4 ....      N—B3
5 P—QB3      Castles

**BLACK**

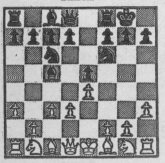

**WHITE**

DIAGRAM 82
(White to play)
Black has developed three pieces and castled his King into safety. White on the other hand has failed to develop a single piece.

White's position in Diagram 82 is really bleak. He has a deficit in development that can never be made up. Not only are all his pieces still on their home squares: it is difficult to see how most of them can reach a good square when they do get out.

But what actually happens in a real game? The following example drastically drives home the consequences of making excessive Pawn moves.

## MUZIO GAMBIT
(Remove White's Queen Rook)
New York, 1859

WHITE      BLACK
*P. Morphy*      *M. D. Conway*

Paul Morphy, as we know, was the most brilliant and most famous master that chess has produced. His emphasis on rapid development revolutionized chess and bridged the gap between modern chess and the chess of the good old days.

In this game Morphy gives the odds of Queen Rook—that is, he plays without this piece. That he can do this and still force checkmate in 12 moves gives us some idea of the disparity in playing strength between the two players.

In addition to giving such enormous odds without the slightest sign of strain, Morphy also sacrifices a Knight and a Bishop. It was this kind of spectacular play that left an indelible impression on the chess world.

|   |   |   |
|---|---|---|
| 1 | P–K4 | P–K4 |
| 2 | P–KB4 | . . . . |

White offers a Pawn in order to get Black's King Pawn out of the way so that he can monopolize the center with a later P–Q4. An opening which involves such a speculative offer of material is known as a "gambit," from an Italian word meaning "to trip up."

|   |   |   |
|---|---|---|
| 2 | . . . . | PxP |

Not a bad move—but he had better start thinking about developing his pieces.

|   |   |   |
|---|---|---|
| 3 | N–KB3 | . . . . |

White's first developing move.

|   |   |   |
|---|---|---|
| 3 | . . . . | P–KN4 |

Dangerous. Instead of developing—say with 3 . . . N–KB3, Black plays still another Pawn move.

|   |   |   |
|---|---|---|
| 4 | B–B4 | . . . . |

Another developing move, and a good one. Note that this Bishop aims menacingly at Black's King Bishop Pawn at King Bishop 2. This is likely to be a weak point early in the game, especially when a player has weakened his position or neglected his development—and Black has done both.

|   |   |   |
|---|---|---|
| 4 | . . . . | P–N5 |

Still another Pawn move—dangerous policy.

DIAGRAM 83
(White to play)
Where should White's
attacked Knight move?

**5 P—Q4!?** . . . .

Secure in the conviction of his enormous superiority, Morphy does not even bother to move his attacked Knight, and instead prefers to build up the pressure. The reader should bear in mind that such cavalier sacrifices are a prerogative of genius and should be strictly left alone by ordinary mortals.

**5** . . . . **PxN**

Black wins more material—but at the cost of making still another Pawn move.

**6 QxP** . . . .

White has a powerful Pawn center and two pieces in play. Already we can sense the build-up of White pressure against Black's Pawn at King Bishop 2.

**6** . . . . **B—R3**

At last Black develops a piece—rather late in the day.

**7 Castles** . . . .

This has a sinister implication here: further strengthening of White's threats on the King Bishop file.

**7** . . . . **N—K2**

Some more belated development—Black hopes to castle, giving his weak King Bishop 2 point some additional protection.

**8  QBxP          BxB**

Now at last the pent-up fury of White's attack breaks out.

DIAGRAM 84
(White to play)
White decides the
game by a startling
sacrifice.

**9  BxPch!      . . . .**

Black cannot very well decline this sacrifice by 9 . . . K—B1, for then White has the winning reply 10 QxB, threatening 11 Q—R6 mate. Then, if Black tries 11 . . . P—KR3, White forces checkmate with 12 B—Q5 dis ch etc.

**9  . . . .        KxB**
**10  QxBch      . . . .**

The brutal attack along the King Bishop file. After 10 . . . K—K3 White has 11 Q—B6 mate.

Another possibility is 10 . . . K—N3; 11 Q—B6ch, K—R4; 12 P—KN4ch, KxP; 13 R—B4ch, K—R4; 14 R—R4 mate.

**10  . . . .       K—N2**
**11  Q—B6ch     K—N1**
**12  Q—B7 mate**

BLACK

WHITE

DIAGONAL 85
(Black is checkmated)
Black's extra pieces
(his Queen Rook,
Queen Knight, Queen
Bishop) were never
developed and played
no role in the whole
game.

This game is a fine example of the harm that can result from excessive Pawn moves and the resulting lack of development. Black's huge advantage in material was meaningless because *he neglected to develop his pieces*.

## DON'T MOVE THE SAME PAWN OR PIECE REPEATEDLY

This is another fault that results in neglected development. Obviously the player who keeps moving the same chessman will never succeed in getting his pieces into action.

Here is a telling example of this faulty type of opening play:

| WHITE | BLACK |
|-------|-------|
| 1 P–K4 | . . . . |

Our approved method of starting the game. Black should follow suit with 1 . . . P–K4. Tchigorin always started his games with 1 P–K4, claiming that this gave him the better game. When he had Black, he answered 1 P–K4 with 1 . . . P–K4, on the theory that this gave him equal chances!

| 1 . . . . | P–KR3? |

A feeble move which does nothing for Black's development.

| 2 P–Q4! | . . . . |

White builds up a powerful Pawn center, monopolizing control of the center squares. Note also that his two Pawn moves have opened diagonals for the development of his Bishops.

                2 . . . .          P—KR4?

Black repeats his previous mistake.

                3 N—KB3          P—R5?

White has developed a piece; Black has continued to move the same Pawn.

                4 B—B4           . . . .

White has developed another piece and is now decidedly ahead in development.

**BLACK**

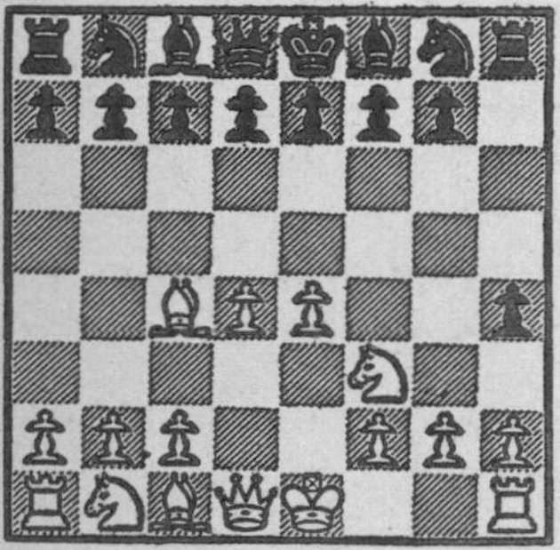

DIAGRAM 86
(Black to play)
Black's repeated moves with the King Rook Pawn have left him hopelessly behind in development.

**WHITE**

Another example of the same fault, this time in moving a piece, is seen in this example:

        WHITE            BLACK
        1  P—K4          P—K4
        2  B—Q3?         . . . .

This is a very poor move because it blocks White's Queen Pawn, making it impossible to develop White's other Bishop. Another drawback of 2 B—Q3? is that the Bishop is deprived of a diagonal by White's King Pawn.

Much more logical is 2 B—B4, which gives the Bishop a splendid diagonal leading down to Black's weak point (King Bishop 2).

                2 . . . .          B—B4

Black, on the other hand, wisely plays his Bishop to the proper square. Now White sees his error and plays:

3   B—B4      . . . .

**BLACK**

DIAGRAM 87
(Black to play)
White has lost a move
by playing 2 B—Q3 and
3 B—B4. (He has
played two moves
where a single move
would have achieved
the very same result.)

**WHITE**

If the game had started 1 P—K4, P—K4; 2 B—B4, B—B4 we would have the position of Diagram 87 with *White to play*. But because White has wasted a whole move, it is *Black's turn to play* in the position of Diagram 87. This is a very simple but significant indication of what happens when the same piece is moved repeatedly.

## AVOID UNDULY PASSIVE MOVES

It is possible to develop one's pieces consistently and yet wind up with a cramped and backward development. How can this be? It comes about from bringing out the pieces timidly and placing them on squares where they have little scope. For example:

| WHITE | BLACK |
|-------|-------|
| 1   P—K4 | P—K4 |
| 2   N—K2? | . . . . |

Feeble. The Knight blocks the development of White's King Bishop and in addition occupies a much less aggressive square than at King Bishop 3.

2   . . . .      N—KB3

Black develops soundly and with gain of time (he attacks White's King Pawn).

3   P–Q3?        ....

Now White's King Bishop, even when it is free to move, will not be able to go very far.

3   ....        B–B4

Another fine developing move. The Bishop has a splendid diagonal, and Black is already threatening to take the initiative with the menacing ... N–N5–aiming at the weak point King Bishop 2.

BLACK

WHITE

DIAGRAM 88
(White to play)
Black has a strong
threat of ... N–N5.

4   N–N3        ....

White moves the Knight a second time. We object to this on principle, but it must be admitted that he doesn't have much choice. By moving the Knight, he prevents 4 ... N–N5. (Why? See Solution L on p. 137.)

In addition, the Knight move makes it possible to develop White's King Bishop.

4   ....        N–B3
5   B–K2        Castles

Black is considerably ahead in development; he has castled his King into safety; his pieces bear effectively on the center, whereas White's pieces seem to have no goals or objectives.

### 6   N—Q2?   . . . .

Another feeble move. The Knight would be better placed at Queen Bishop 3, where it has a stronger role in the center. Also, at Queen 2 this Knight blocks the development of White's Queen Bishop.

### 6   . . . .   P—Q3

Black opens the diagonal for his Queen Bishop.

### 7   N—N3   . . . .

Again White moves a Knight a second time. But he can hardly help himself, as he wishes to open his Queen Bishop's diagonal.

### 7   . . . .   B—N3!

It is true that Black is making a second move with this Bishop, but he has an overriding purpose. The exchange of Knight for Bishop would leave the players even in material, but it would nevertheless be in White's favor.

This is based on a general principle: When a player has a cramped position, it is to his advantage to lighten the pressure by seeking exchanges. Conversely, when a player has an advantage in space, he runs the danger of dissipating that advantage by allowing exchanges.

The moral is clear: Black has no intention of allowing his well-placed Bishop to be exchanged for White's badly placed Knight.

### 8   Castles   B—K3

**BLACK**

**WHITE**

DIAGRAM 89
(White to play)
Thanks to his far superior development, Black has much the better game. White is definitely on the defensive.

## AVOID PREMATURE QUEEN MOVES

For many inexperienced players, early Queen moves have an irresistible fascination. Some are attracted by the Queen's power to make long-range moves; others send the Queen on far-flung journeys to win a comparatively unimportant Pawn.

What is generally not realized is that the Queen is vulnerable precisely because of her value and power. When attacked by protected Pawns and pieces, the Queen has no alternative to an inglorious retreat. The following game plausibly demonstrates what can happen to the Queen on one of these ill-judged excursions.

### CENTER COUNTER GAME

| | WHITE | BLACK |
|---|---|---|
| 1 | P–K4 | P–Q4 |

This move is generally frowned upon because it results in Black's Queen coming into play prematurely.

| | | |
|---|---|---|
| 2 | PxP | QxP |
| 3 | N–QB3 | . . . . |

There we have it. White's Knight develops with gain of time by attacking Black's Queen.

BLACK

WHITE

DIAGRAM 90
(Black to play)
Black must move his
Queen out of danger.

3 .... Q–K4ch

Doubtless the most obvious reply. But the Black Queen is still exposed to attack.

4 B–K2 N–KB3
5 N–B3 ....

Once more White develops with gain of time by attacking the Black Queen.

5 .... Q–Q3
6 Castles ....

Thanks to Black's faulty Queen moves, White has an enormous lead in development.

6 .... P–K4

Black wants to gain time to play ... B–K2 followed by castling.

7 N–QN5 ....

White continues to hound the Queen, which must move to a square where she prevents NxBPch forking Black's King and his Queen Rook. In addition, the Queen must continue to guard the King Pawn.

7 .... Q–B4
8 P–QN4! ....

Still hounding the Black Queen.

BLACK

DIAGRAM 91
(Black to play)
Black must not play 8
... QxNP? Why? (See
Solution M on p.
137.)

WHITE

|    |        |          |
|----|--------|----------|
| 8  | . . . .| Q–N3     |
| 9  | NxKP   | BxP      |
| 10 | N–B4   | . . . .  |

The attacks on the Queen continue. Black can eke out a miserable existence with 10 . . . Q–B3, but instead he falls victim to a trap.

|    |         |          |
|----|---------|----------|
| 10 | . . . . | QxN?     |
| 11 | N–Q6ch  | Resigns  |

Black's Queen is attacked not only by White's Knight but also by his Bishop on King 2. But since Black is in check, he has no time to save his Queen.

**BLACK**

DIAGRAM 92
(Black to play)
Black's Queen is lost.

**WHITE**

When an inexperienced player loses a game in this drastic fashion, we take it as a matter of course. But when this happens to a recognized master of some standing, then it is a cause for wonderment. Here is a game in which an international master loses his Queen in eight moves!

### SCOTCH GAME
Paris, 1888

| WHITE      | BLACK          |
|------------|----------------|
| *Frazer*   | *J. Taubenhaus*|

|   |        |        |
|---|--------|--------|
| 1 | P–K4   | P–K4   |
| 2 | N–KB3  | N–QB3  |

White has attacked Black's King Pawn; Black has defended it. Both players have started with good developing moves.

3    P—Q4        . . . .

This move is not a blunder, but it is not the best. It is good in that it takes an aggressive position in the center and opens up the diagonal of White's Queen Bishop.

But 3 P—Q4 also has a drawback, as will become clear on the next move.

3    . . . .        PxP

This is Black's simplest reply to White's threat to win a Pawn.

4    NxP        . . . .

Here is the drawback to this opening, as far as White is concerned. In order to win back his Pawn, White has to move the Knight *a second time*. In effect he has lost a move, giving Black a chance to seize the initiative.

We must conclude, then, that after 1 P—K4, P—K4; 2 N—KB3, N—QB3 White's best course is to play a developing move, such as 3 B—N5 or 3 B—B4.

BLACK

DIAGRAM 93
(Black to play)
Black can take the initiative with a well-considered developing move.

WHITE

Black can now develop advantageously with 4 . . . B—B4 or 4 . . . N—B3. After either of these moves, we find that White has developed only one piece, while Black has developed two! Here you again have proof that White's combination of 3 P—Q4 and 4 NxP has cost him a move. This is an example of an opening fault we studied earlier—moving the same piece twice.

And now note this: if Black plays 4 . . . B—B4 he is threatening to win a piece. If he plays 4 . . . N—B3 he is threatening to win a Pawn. In either case, we see how neglected development puts a player on the defensive, whereas consistent development is likely to give him the initiative.

Now we return to the position of Diagram 93.

$$4 \ldots \ldots \quad Q\text{—}R5?$$

This move attacks White's King Pawn, but we are going to dismiss it on principle because it violates the rules of good development. We know that the premature development of Black's Queen should lead to trouble for him.

$$5 \ N\text{—}QB3 \quad \ldots \ldots$$

White develops a piece and at the same time protects his attacked King Pawn.

$$5 \ldots \ldots \quad N\text{—}B3$$

Black attacks the King Pawn again, also by a developing move. But at the same time he creates a subtle danger for himself: *he cuts off his Queen's retreat.*

$$6 \ N\text{—}B5! \quad \ldots \ldots$$

White loses no time in seizing his opportunity.

BLACK

DIAGRAM 94
(Black to play)
Black's Queen is in terrible danger.

WHITE

Black sees that his Queen is attacked, but he fails to realize that he is only a hairline from disaster.

6  . . . .          Q—R4??

Reckoning only on 7 QxQ, NxQ etc., Black has overlooked that his Queen will now be trapped.

7  B—K2!          . . . .

The Bishop develops with a gain of time—and what a gain of time! Black's Queen has only one move.

7  . . . .          Q—N3
8  N—KR4!          Resigns

**BLACK**

DIAGRAM 95
(Black to play)
Black's Queen is
trapped!

**WHITE**

Show that Black loses his Queen after such moves as 8 . . . Q—R3 or 8 . . . Q—N4 or 8 . . . QxKP or 8 . . . QxNP. (See Solution N on p. 137.)

## DON'T EXPOSE YOUR KING TO ATTACK

Since the King's well-being is the crucial factor in chess, this vital piece should be strongly protected as a matter of course. Yet, surprising as it may seem, players often neglect this all-important phase of the game and carelessly open the gates to the enemy. It is literally the surest way to defeat.

Here is what happens when a very weak player presents opportunities to a great master of attack.

### CENTER GAME
Vienna, 1936

#### (Simultaneous Exhibition)

| WHITE | BLACK |
|-------|-------|
| *A. Alekhine* | *Amateur* |

Many years ago I paid tribute to Alekhine's genius in these words:

"Alekhine's style was so forceful, so brilliant, so resourceful that his games are the most fascinating that any man has produced. It is difficult to conceive the advent of a superman who will excel Alekhine in tactical skill. No master, of any period whatever, even remotely approaches Alekhine in the consistency, artistry, profundity and dramatic richness of his achievements."

Yet, for all his daring at the chessboard, he was burdened with strangely timorous quirks of character. After fleeing from Russia in 1921 he had lived in great poverty for some time in Germany. This harrowing period left a lifelong mark on him. I can vividly recall meeting him for the first time at the Pasadena tournament of 1932, for my naïve, hero-worshiping attitude was jarred by some of his strange whims. For example, although he was virtually a chain-smoker, he always kept his cigarettes in his pocket. When he wanted to smoke, he would reach into his pocket and maneuver one cigarette out without removing the pack. In this way he avoided the social necessity of offering his companion or opponent a cigarette!

See if you can recognize this strange neurotic in the following game:

| | | |
|---|---|---|
| 1 | P–K4 | P–K4 |
| 2 | P–Q4 | .... |

Instead of developing a piece, White has immediately pushed forward in the center. This is questionable policy, for Black can simply play 2 ... PxP; then, after the indicated

BLACK

WHITE

DIAGRAM 96
(Black to play)
Does this position
remind you of the
situation in Diagram
90?

reply 3 QxP, we find that White's Queen has entered the fray prematurely. This gives Black an opportunity to counter advantageously with 3 . . . ? (See Solution O on p. 137.)

Instead of playing to gain the initiative, Black heads for trouble with:

2  . . . .  P–KB3?

This is a bad move primarily because it opens up the approaches to Black's King. We have seen in earlier examples that the uncastled King is particularly sensitive to pressure on the King Bishop 2 square, and this situation is no exception to the general rule.

3  PxP  PxP??

If Black had had any idea of what was coming, he would have given up a Pawn, say with some such developing move as 3 . . . N–B3. Instead, he subjects himself to a devastating attack.

4  Q–R5ch!  . . . .

The refutation, but it requires some explaining. Generally an early Queen move is premature; in this case the move is not premature because the Queen check has a very concrete and valuable purpose: to force Black to move his King.

BLACK

DIAGRAM 97
(Black to play)
Why is 4 . . . P–KN3
unsatisfactory for
Black? (See Solution
P on p. 137.)

WHITE

4 . . . .          K–K2

A disastrous situation for Black. His King is now exposed
to an endless series of damaging checks and threats.

5  QxKPch        K–B2
6  B–QB4ch       . . . .

White develops the Bishop with gain of time. Is 6 . . .
K–N3 feasible? (See Solution Q on p. 137.)

6  . . . .        P–Q4
7  BxPch          K–N3
8  Q–N3ch         K–R4

Black is paying a heavy price for neglecting the safety of
his King. (If instead 8 . . . K–B3 White replies 9 Q–KN5
mate.)

9  B–B7ch         P–KN3
10  P–KR3!        . . . .

This innocent-looking move involves a brutal threat. See
Diagram 98.

10  . . . .        Q–B3

This blocks White's checkmate threat. Why? (See Solution
R on p. 137.)

BLACK

WHITE

DIAGRAM 98
(Black to play)
White's amazing threat
is:
    11  Q—N4ch!!  BxQ
    12  PxB dbl ch  KxP
    13  B—K6 mate!
A very beautiful
checkmate.

### 11  N—KB3!    . . . .

Now Black must not play 11 . . . QxBPP because of the reply 12 P (See Solution S on p. 138.)

Meanwhile White has stubbornly renewed his mate threat, the idea now being 12 Q—N4ch!!, BxQ; 13 PxB dbl ch, KxP; 14 B—K6ch! (a nice point), QxB; 15 R—R4 mate.

### 11  . . . .    B—K2

Played to parry the R—R4 mate possibility (see the end of the previous note).

But Alekhine has the last word anyway by announcing mate in six moves. Beautiful as his checkmate is, we have to bear in mind that it is made possible only by Black's slovenly neglect of his King's safety.

Here is the announced mate:

### 12  Q—N4ch!!    . . . .

White's insistence on this idea lends an impish touch to the game.

    12  . . . .    BxQ
    13  PxB dbl ch    KxP
    14  N—R2ch!    . . . .

A move which shows extraordinary powers of imagination. It is difficult to realize that White can still force the mate after seeming to allow Black's King to escape.

14  . . . .          K—R4

After 14 . . . K—R5 White forces mate the same way.

15  N—B1ch          . . . .

**BLACK**

**WHITE**

DIAGRAM 99
(Black to move)
If Black plays 15 . . .
Q—R5, White mates in
two moves. How? (See
Solution T on p. 138.)

15  . . . .          K—N5
16  B—K6ch!          . . . .

To entice Black's Queen away from the main scene of action.

16  . . . .          QxB
17  P—KB3 mate

What heightens the piquancy of this exquisite mate is the fact that all of White's pieces are on the back row. But Black's King is far from home—and helpless.


## ADDITIONAL GAMES—
## THE PSYCHOLOGICAL FACTOR

The three games which conclude this chapter are by way of review, as they illustrate familiar faulty ways of playing the opening. But the instructive feature is really psychological—in each case the loser deceives himself about the real nature of the situation.

## SICILIAN DEFENSE
### Essen, 1948

| WHITE | BLACK |
|-------|-------|
| *L. Schmid* | *W. Sahlmann* |

| | | |
|---|---|---|
| 1 | P–K4 | P–QB4 |

Black deviates from our recommended 1 . . . P–K4. His actual move is quite playable, as it is directed against White's hope of monopolizing the center with P–Q4.

| | | |
|---|---|---|
| 2 | N–KB3 | P–Q3 |
| 3 | P–Q4 | PxP |
| 4 | NxP | P–KN3 |

Black intends to play his King Bishop to King Knight 2, in the hope of controlling the long diagonal and thereby the center.

| | | |
|---|---|---|
| 5 | P–QB4 | N–KB3 |

Black attacks White's King Pawn.

| | | |
|---|---|---|
| 6 | N–QB3 | N–B3 |
| 7 | P–B3 | . . . . |

The logical course for Black is now 7 . . . B–N2, completing the development of his King-side pieces and preparing to castle.

Instead, Black is carried away by the idea of developing his Queen prematurely.

| | | |
|---|---|---|
| 7 | . . . . | Q–N3? |

BLACK

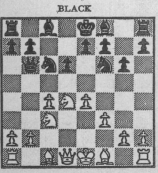

WHITE

DIAGRAM 100
(White to play)
Black is courting trouble with his early development of the Queen.

On the face of it, 7 . . . Q—N3? has many attractive features. It attacks White's Knight at Queen 4 doubly and therefore threatens to win a piece. If White replies 8 NxN Black
recaptures with 8 . . . PxN with a splendid game: open Queen
Knight file, open long diagonal for his King Bishop from King
Knight 2 and another fine diagonal for his Queen (for example, after White develops his King Bishop he will be unable
to castle).

It is true that White can reply 8 N—N3, but then Black
simply follows up with 8 . . . B—N2 with very strong diagonal
pressure.

And of course 8 B—K3 is ruled out by the reply 8 . . .
QxP winning a Pawn and attacking a White Knight.

### 8   B—K3!!         . . . .

But this unexpected reply is not ruled out at all, as White
cleverly demonstrates.

BLACK

DIAGRAM 101
(Black to play)
Black can play 8 . . .
QxP and gain time
by attacking one of
White's Knights. Is the
capture advisable?

WHITE

There are some very instructive possibilities here. For
example, if Black plays 8 . . . P—K4 White must not play
9 NxN?, for then Black wins a piece. (How? See Solution U
on p. 138.)

Instead, after 8 . . . P—K4 White plays 9 N—B2 attacking
the Black Queen. If Black is then incautious enough to grab
a Pawn (9 . . . QxP??) White plays 10 N—N5 with two
frightful threats. (What are they? See Solution V on p. 138.)
As Black would be unable to parry *both* threats, he would
have a definitely lost game.

Now here is where the psychological factor enters. Black would be well advised to swallow his pride and retreat 8 . . . Q—Q1. But this would be confessing failure, not to mention the loss of two moves. White would simply continue 9 Q—Q2, with a fine lead in development.

Hoping, therefore, to salvage something from his investment in the Queen moves, Black continues plausibly with:

$$8 \ldots \ldots \qquad \text{QxP??}$$

A ruinous capture. Black's Queen is now lost!

$$9 \ \text{N—R4!} \qquad \text{Q—R6}$$

Or 9 . . . Q—N5ch; 10 B—Q2 and Black's Queen is trapped in the same way as in the actual continuation.

$$10 \ \text{B—B1!} \qquad \ldots \ldots$$

Black's Queen is left with only one move.

$$10 \ldots \ldots \qquad \text{Q—N5ch}$$
$$11 \ \text{B—Q2} \qquad \ldots \ldots$$

Again leaving the Queen only one move. This is a highly instructive example of what happens when the Queen, after being developed prematurely, indulges in indiscriminate Pawn-hunting.

$$11 \ldots \ldots \qquad \text{Q—R6}$$

Once more a forced move. But the Queen's unlucky career now comes to an end.

$$12 \ \text{N—N5} \qquad \text{Resigns}$$

Rather than lose his Queen for a Knight, Black rightly surrenders. Prove that his Queen is trapped. (See Solution W on p. 138.)

Perhaps the most important lesson of all that this game teaches is to beware of that very common chess maxim, "A bad plan is better than none at all." Certainly Black's bad plan (early development of the Queen) did not confer any blessing.

In the following game White loses quickly not so much because of a bad plan but rather because of feeble execution of a good plan.

### FRENCH DEFENSE
Berlin, 1920

| WHITE | BLACK |
|-------|-------|
| *Seppelt* | *Laeganki* |

| 1  P–K4 | P–K3 |

BLACK

WHITE

DIAGRAM 102
(White to play)
Now that Black has
avoided the more
common 1 . . . P–K4,
we must ask ourselves:
What is his plan for
fighting for Pawn
control of the center?

At first sight 1 . . . P–K3 seems a serious strategical
blunder, as White can reply 2 P–Q4 monopolizing the Pawn
center. But then Black alertly counters with 2 . . . P–Q4,
which gives him a vital foothold in the center after all.

But 1 . . . P–K3 does involve a drawback which may involve Black in serious trouble later on: this Pawn move blocks
the natural diagonal of Black's Queen Bishop. If Black is a
good player he will be aware of this difficulty and will bend
his energies to finding some way to solve it. But if he is an
inexperienced player, he will not be aware of his disability.

2    P–Q4      . . . .

White's indicated advance in the center.

2  . . . .      P–Q4

Black's indicated counterplay in the center.
Now we find that Black's challenge in the center poses a

problem for White, in that his King Pawn is attacked. The simplest way to solve the problem—but not the best way— is to play 3 PxP. But then, after 3 . . . PxP, we have a symmetrical position, which indicates to us that White has made no headway. In addition, *the diagonal of Black's Queen Bishop has been opened up,* removing Black's main problem in this opening.

White can also push by: 3 P–K5. This has a cramping effect on Black's game; for example, his Queen Bishop is now locked in and his Knight cannot go to King Bishop 3. On the other hand, Black has good counterplay in 3 . . . P–QB4, counterattacking against White's Queen Pawn which defends his advanced King Pawn.

So White's final alternative course—to guard his King Pawn *with a developing move*—seems to make the most sense. The logical move in that case is to play 3 N–QB3, guarding the King Pawn and putting White's Queen Knight on his best square.

Instead, White plays:

3   N–Q2     . . . .

BLACK

WHITE

DIAGRAM 103
(Black to play)
Can you see why
White's actual move
(3 N–Q2) is inferior
to the recommended
move (3 N–QB3)?

The moves 3 N–QB3 and 3 N–Q2 are of equal value in that each one protects White's King Pawn. There the equality ends. For 3 N–Q2 is inferior in two vital respects.

In the first place, 3 N–QB3 is more aggressive: it exercises pressure on squares on the fifth rank, whereas 3 N—Q2 only exercises pressure on squares on the fourth rank.

The other and even worse drawback of 3 N—Q2 is that it blocks the development of White's Queen Bishop. So we see that 3 N—Q2 is unduly passive and self-limiting.

If Black is well aware of these drawbacks to 3 N—Q2, the last move he will think of is 3 . . . PxP. For after the reply 4 NxP the Knight is excellently placed in the center and no longer blocks the White Queen Bishop. (This is a good example of the way that the effects of a weak move can be nullified by a weak reply.)

3 . . . .          P—QB4!

Excellent. If Black succeeds in removing the White Queen Pawn, his pieces will have more scope in the center.

4 KPxP          . . . .

Here is where the psychological factor enters. White is playing to give his opponent an isolated Queen Pawn. (This will be explained in the next note.)

4 . . . .          KPxP
5 PxP          BxP

BLACK

DIAGRAM 104
(White to play)
White has carried out his plan, but Black has a very promising position.

WHITE

White has succeeded in giving Black an isolated Queen Pawn. This is a Pawn which cannot be protected by its neighboring Pawns, which have disappeared by capture. The point is that such a Pawn has to be protected by pieces and therefore frequently turns out to be a serious weakness.

Such refined strategy has worked very well in the games of the great masters, but we are not concerned with that here. White is just a weak player who ought to be thinking of how to develop his pieces and how to guard his King against any lurking danger; instead, he is preoccupied with elaborate plans that require enormous ability and experience for their successful execution.

The fact that Black's Queen Bishop was released by the exchange on move 4 is certainly a plus for Black. The fact that his King Bishop has taken up a powerful diagonal (remember Diagram 84?) is another plus for him.

If White is aware of the potential dangers he will play 6 B—N5ch (developing a King-side piece), B—Q2; 7 BxBch, NxB; 8 KN—B3 (developing another King-side piece). Now he is prepared to castle and all's well—or reasonably so.

Instead, White commits a fearful blunder.

**6  N—K2??       . . . .**

Had White been familiar with the general rule against playing a Knight to the second rank instead of the third, he could have avoided this move even without seeing its damaging consequences.

He is now helpless against the following attack on his King Bishop Pawn—or King Bishop 2 square.

**6  . . . .          Q—N3!**
Resigns

BLACK

DIAGRAM 105
(White to play)
White can stop the threatened mate only by incurring ruinous material loss.

WHITE

Black of course threatens 7 . . . BxP mate. The unfortunate position of White's Knights robs him of any worthwhile defensive tries.

Nor is it possible to give White's King a flight square by moving the Queen Knight. For example, after 7 N—QN3 or 7 N—KB3 we get 7 . . . BxPch; 8 K—Q2, Q—K6 mate. Likewise after 7 N—KN3 or 7 N—QB3 the inexorable answer is 7 . . . BxPch; 8 K—K2, Q—K6 mate.

So White must play 7 N—Q4, BxN; 8 N—B3, BxPch; 9 K—K2. But then the win is child's play for Black, who is a Knight and Pawn ahead.

White sadly overreached himself by ignoring the homely, basic rules of effective development and striving for highfalutin strategical conceptions.

It seems appropriate to conclude this chapter with a game of the great Paul Morphy, who was the first to stress the all-important principle of rapid and effective development. It is interesting that Morphy never gave a public explanation of this concept. It is doubly interesting that the following game was played by him at the age of twelve. This proves that the principle of rapid development, which was to have a lasting effect on the way that chess is played, must have been acquired instinctively by him.


EVANS GAMBIT
New Orleans, 1849

WHITE          BLACK
*P. Morphy*      *A. Morphy*


1  P—K4          P—K4


Apparently this game was played at a time when young Paul still had to sit on a fat book in order to be able to reach comfortably across the board—as when he plays 21 R—B8 mate in this game. His opponent here is one of his uncles, Alonzo Morphy.


2  N—KB3          N—QB3
3  B—B4           B—B4
4  P—QN4          . . . .

BLACK

WHITE

DIAGRAM 106
(Black to play)
White plays a "gambit"
—he gives up a Pawn in
order to gain time for
attack.

4 .... BxNP

Of course, this acceptance of the gambit is by no means necessarily fatal, as Black has plenty of resources for defense if he plays properly.

The prudent course is doubtless 4 . . . B—N3, spurning the gambit Pawn and maintaining a perfectly safe position. But here the psychological factor comes into play again—in the days when this game was played it was considered unsportsmanlike to turn down a gambit Pawn.

5 P—B3      B—B4
6 P—Q4      ....

By attacking Black's Bishop White gains time to build up a strong center.

6 ....      PxP
7 PxP       B—N3
8 Castles   ....

White's position is more comfortable, but the game is far from being won.

8 ....      N—R4

Black moves the Knight a second time—after moving his Bishop four times, a warning signal. But he wants to remove White's Bishop from its commanding post at Queen Bishop 4.

9 B—Q3      ....

BLACK

DIAGRAM 107
(Black to play)
Should Black advance
his Queen Pawn one
square or two?

WHITE

The general rule in such situations is: If you have a greater command of the board, open up new lines of attack so that your pieces can function even more actively. On the other hand, if you have less command of the board, try to keep the position closed so that your opening will not obtain new avenues of attack.

How does this apply to the situation in Diagram 107? After 9 . . . P–Q4 White will obtain new lines of attack; after 9 . . . P–Q3 he will not. Hence 9 . . . P–Q3 is the right move.

| 9 | . . . . | P–Q4? |
| 10 | PxP | QxP |
| 11 | B–R3! | . . . . |

Now see what harm Black has done to his prospects. Not only does White have the open King file available for attack; he also has a clear diagonal for his Queen Bishop leading down to King Bishop 8. In short: Black is lost.

|  | 11 . . . . | B–K3 |

Black makes a futile attempt to close up the King file which he has so foolishly opened.

At first sight it seems that Black could have gained more material with 11 . . . BxP. Is this correct? (See Solution X on p. 138.)

|  | 12 N–B3 | . . . . |

By attacking Black's Queen, White gains time for development.

|  | 12 . . . . | Q–Q2 |

BLACK

DIAGRAM 108
(White to play)
How does White force
open new attacking
lines?

WHITE

If Black is given a chance, he will now castle Queen-side, getting his King out of immediate danger, with a fair chance of survival. So time is of the essence. This is the kind of position in which Morphy was always at his best.

13    P—Q5!    . . . .

The Morphy trade-mark—a Pawn sacrifice to open attacking lines. Whether or not Black captures, White gets in a wicked check on the King file.

13    . . . .    BxQP
14    NxB    QxN
15    B—N5ch!!    . . . .

A very beautiful move—especially coming from a child. Black must capture. Show that 15 . . . P—QB3? is an altogether unsatisfactory reply. (See Solution Y on p. 138.)

15    . . . .    QxB
16    R—K1ch    . . . .

This attack on the exposed Black King must be decisive.

16    . . . .    N—K2

Now White has an easy win with 17 RxNch, K—B1; 18 R—N1! Black cannot reply 18 . . . Q—B3 or 18 . . . Q—B5 as White would then win Black's Queen. HOW? (See Solution Z on p. 138.)

Consequently, after 17 RxNch, K—B1; 18 R—N1! Black

has nothing better than 18 . . . Q–R3 after which 19 Q–Q5 is murderous.

17  R–N1?!        ≋ ≋ ≋ ≋

**BLACK**

DIAGRAM 109
(Black to play)
With best play Black
can still put up
substantial resistance.

**WHITE**

A pardonable lapse in a youngster. He gives Black a chance to put up a fight with 17 . . . Q–Q2; 18 RxNch, QxR; 19 BxQ, KxB etc.

17  . . . .        Q–R3?
18  RxNch        . . . .

Now White's train is on the right track again.

18  . . . .        K–B1
19  Q–Q5          . . . .

White's chief threat is 20 ? (See Solution AA on p. 138.)

19  . . . .        Q–B5
20  RxKBP dbl ch   K–N1

In the event of 20 . . . K–K1 White replies 21 ? (See Solution BB on p. 138.)

21  R–B8 mate

An attractive double check provides an elegant finish.

From your study of these brief but very instructive games you have obtained a clear insight into the vital importance of developing your pieces in the opening. You have seen that the pieces must come out quickly—that they must be placed effectively on posts from which they can function actively. You have also come to realize that pieces posted in the center are likely to be at their best.

These games have shown you the harmful effects of too many Pawn moves, of excessive moves with the same Pawn or piece. They have demonstrated the need for early castling as a protection for the King, and they have shown the dangers which surround a King exposed to hostile attack.

On the positive side these games have revealed the ease with which strong moves turn up in good positions, and the likelihood that good plans present themselves readily when the pieces have been developed satisfactorily.

The moral should not be forgotten when you play your own games. Concentrate on rapid, effective development and you will be well repaid in satisfying results.

# 4

# THE BASIC PRINCIPLE
# OF ENDGAME PLAY

The endgame is just that—the "end of the game." Assume that you have won material—a Pawn, several Pawns, maybe a piece. Many of the chessmen have disappeared from the board. What then?

In some cases you may be down to one of the basic checkmates, in which your opponent is left with nothing but his King. Here are the minimum forces with which checkmate can be achieved:

King and Queen against King (Diagrams 17, 18).
King and Rook against King (Diagram 18).
King and two Bishops against King (Diagram 19).
King and Bishop and Knight against King (Diagram 20).

Suppose you are left with King and Knight against King, or with Bishop against King? Then the game is a draw, as has been pointed out earlier.

BLACK

WHITE

DIAGRAM 110a
White's material
advantage is useless.
The position is a draw.

Now let's make a slight change in Diagram 110a, adding a White Pawn. This gives us the situation of Diagram 110b.

**BLACK**

**WHITE**

**DIAGRAM 110b**
White has an easy win,
no matter whose move
it is.

If it is White's move, play might proceed as follows:

| WHITE | | BLACK |
|---|---|---|
| 1 | N–Q5ch | K–Q2 |
| 2 | P–K6ch | K–K1 |
| 3 | K–B6 | K–Q1 |
| 4 | P–K7ch | . . . . |

White can also win with 4 K–B7 followed by the further
advance of the Pawn.

| | | |
|---|---|---|
| 4 | . . . . | K–K1 |
| 5 | N–B7ch | K–Q2 |
| 6 | P–K8/Qch | . . . . |

And White will force checkmate with his new Queen (the
standard ending of King and Queen against King).

So there you have the difference between Diagram 110a
and Diagram 110b. *The Pawn—every Pawn—is a potential
Queen.* This is the basic principle of endgame play.

Here is another ending which illustrates the same principle:

In Diagram 111 White has an easy win. Play might proceed:

| WHITE | | BLACK |
|---|---|---|
| 1 | K–Q6 dis ch | K–N3 |
| 2 | B–K6 | K–R3 |
| 3 | K–K7 | K–N3 |
| 4 | B–B5ch | K–N2 |
| 5 | K–K6 | K moves |
| 6 | KxP | . . . . |

BLACK

WHITE

**DIAGRAM 111**
(White to play)
Without White's Pawn
the ending would be a
draw; with the Pawn,
White wins easily.

And White wins easily by escorting his Pawn to the queening square.

Of course the extra piece is often not needed to score the win. Most endings of King and Pawn against King are won for the player with the extra Pawn. Take Diagram 112 as an example.

BLACK

WHITE

**DIAGRAM 112**
(White to play)
White wins.

White wins by advancing the Pawn:

| WHITE | BLACK |
|-------|-------|
| 1 P–K7 | K–B2 |
| 2 K–Q7 | . . . . |

White's next move will be 3 P—K8/Q and wins.

The winning procedure in Diagram 113a is a little more elaborate.

BLACK

WHITE

DIAGRAM 113a
(White to play)
White wins.

White aims for the winning situation of Diagram 112:

| WHITE | | BLACK |
|-------|------|-------|
| 1 | K—Q6 | K—K1 |
| 2 | P—K7 | K—B2 |
| 3 | K—Q7 | . . . . |

And again White forces the queening of his Pawn.

The situation in Diagram 113b is tricky.

BLACK

WHITE

DIAGRAM 113b
(White to play)
1 P—K6? only draws
for White. But 1
K—K6! wins.

First we examine the consequences of 1 P—K6?

| WHITE | BLACK |
|-------|-------|
| 1  P—K6? | K—Q1 |
| 2  P—K7ch | K—K1 |
| 3  K—K6 | Drawn |

Black is stalemated!
Now for the right way (from Diagram 113a).

| 1  K—K6! | K—Q1 |
|----------|------|

On 1 . . . K—B1 White wins with 2 K—Q7.

| 2  K—B7 | K—Q2 |
|---------|------|
| 3  P—K6ch | K—Q1 |
| 4  P—K7ch | . . . . |

And White succeeds in queening his Pawn.

Diagram 114 illustrates the effectiveness of the "outside passed Pawn."

BLACK

DIAGRAM 114
(White to play)
Though material is even, an experienced player can see at a glance that White has a won game.

WHITE

A passed Pawn is one that is unopposed by a hostile Pawn on its own file or neighboring files. White's Rook Pawn is a passed Pawn. Such Pawns have a special value because their advance can be held back only by pieces. A passed Pawn, by its very nature, is so to speak halfway on the way to becoming a Queen. Such a Pawn is a standing menace to the opponent, who must employ one or more pieces to keep this Pawn from queening.

Diagram 114 is a fine example of the power of a passed Pawn. Material is even, and this might lead an inexperienced player to conclude that the players have equal prospects.

An experienced player, however, can recognize at a single glance that White has an easily won game. Why is this so? It is White's passed Rook Pawn—an "outside passed Pawn" —that makes all the difference. On the King-side Black's two Pawns are effectively restrained by a single White Pawn. The Black Pawns are *fixed* on their present squares.

In order to win, White must carry out the maneuver K—B6—N7. Momentarily this is blocked by Black's King. But Black's King can be enticed away from the critical zone by a timely advance of White's menacing passed Pawn. So White's indicated course is very clear:

| WHITE | BLACK |
|---|---|
| 1  P—R5! | . . . . |

White threatens to queen this Pawn. Black is forced to bring his king over.

| 1 . . . . | K—Q2 |
|---|---|

But now Black is vulnerable to the following invasion:

| 2  K—B6 | . . . . |
|---|---|

Black is powerless. The ending might wind up in the following manner:

| 2 . . . . | K—B3 |
|---|---|
| 3  K—N7 | K—N4 |
| 4  KxP | KxP |
| 5  KxP | Resigns |

White will queen his remaining Pawn.

## ENDINGS WITH PIECES AND PAWNS

With more pieces on the board the endings become more complex, but the basic principle remains the same: The advantage of an extra Pawn or a passed Pawn generally proves decisive. The implied threat of queening such a Pawn is the motif that assures the victory of the superior side. An important winning technique is for the stronger side to threaten exchanges that would lead to an easily won King and Pawn ending. The situation in Diagram 115 instructively highlights these features of endgame play.

BLACK

WHITE

DIAGRAM 115
(Black to play)
Which passed Pawn is
more dangerous?

The position of Diagram 115 arose in a match game played at Paris in 1858 between Harrwitz (White) and Paul Morphy (Black). While Morphy's great fame rests primarily on his prowess as a brilliant player, he was also a superlative master of endgame technique, as we shall note from his splendid handling of this rather puzzling situation.

Black is a Pawn ahead, to be sure, but this is not important for the moment. The play centers about the two passed Pawns, both of which look quite menacing. White, for example, threatens P—B7, after which the Pawn cannot be stopped from queening.

Black's passed Pawn, on the other hand, seems less threatening, for after 1 . . . P—B7 White simply plays 2 K—Q2. But this is just where Morphy's genius shines in the brightest light, for he shows convincingly that the situation is not so simple after all.

| WHITE | BLACK |
|-------|-------|
| 1 . . . . | P—B7! |

This is the right move after all. If White tries 2 P—B7 there follows 2 . . . P—B8/Q; 3 P—B8/Q, R—R7ch and Black mates in two moves.

2 K—Q2 . . . .

The obvious (and seemingly excellent) alternative.

                    2 ....              R—B6!

Beautiful play. Black threatens to queen his Pawn and
thus he gains time to confiscate White's dangerous Pawn.
Clearly White cannot play 3 KxR allowing 3 . . . P—B8/Qch
with an easy win for Black.

                    3 K—B1              ....

Forced.

                    3 ....              RxBP

Here is an instructive moment. White is two Pawns down,
but he can win back one of them by playing 4 R—N2 and
5 RxP. However, the resulting King and Pawn ending would
be an easy win for Black, as we shall see later on.

                    4 R—N3              K—B3

Black's King must force an entry on the King-side. The key
to this process is . . . P—N4, which is prepared by the King
move.

                    5 R—R3              P—N4

This threatens 6 . . . PxP which, after White's recapture,
will give Black three connected passed Pawns—an easy win.
On the other hand, if White plays 6 PxPch there follows
6 . . . KxP and then 7 . . . P—B5, achieving the same result.

                    6 P—N3              ....

The idea is to answer 6 . . . NPxP with 7 NPxP, preventing
Black from getting his passed Pawns. But now Black will
soon be ready to play . . . K—N3—R4—N5—B6.

                    6 ....              RPxP
                    7 RPxP              PxP
                    8 NPxP              K—N3

Suppose White hits on the idea of keeping his Rook on
the third rank to guard his King Pawn. Then Black still wins
in the following manner: 9 R—N3, K—R4; 10 R—R3, K—N5;
11 R—N3, K—B6; 12 R—R3, K—B7; 13 R—N3, P—Q4!; 14
R—R3, P—Q5! Black forces a new passed Pawn, which wins
very quickly by virtue of the queening threat. There follows

BLACK

WHITE

DIAGRAM 116
(White to play)
Will passive play hold
the position for White?

15 PxP, P—K6 and White must give up his Rook for the Pawn.

Now back to Diagram 116.

|    |       |       |
|----|-------|-------|
| 9  | R—R5  | R—B4  |
| 10 | R—R6  | R—B6  |
| 11 | RxPch | K—R4  |
| 12 | R—Q2  | K—N5  |

An instructive situation. White has regained a Pawn and can win a second one with 13 RxP. But after 13 . . . RxRch!; 14 KxR, K—B6; 15 K—Q2, K—B7 Black picks up both White Pawns and wins with ease.

13 R—N2ch

Or 13 R—K2, K—B6; 14 R—K1, K—B7 again with an easy win for Black.

|    |        |       |
|----|--------|-------|
| 13 | . . . . | K—B6  |
| 14 | R—N5   | R—B4  |
| 15 | R—R5   | KxP   |
| 16 | R—R4   | K—B6  |
|    | Resigns |       |

A very convincing example of the power of passed Pawns. There are situations in which a passed Pawn is so formidable that it is worth sacrificing a piece to get the passed Pawn. Diagram 117 is a good example.

BLACK

WHITE

DIAGRAM 117
(Black to play)
How can Black obtain
a powerful passed
Pawn?

This colorless-looking position seems perfectly level; yet with the Black pieces handled by a great master (Capablanca), we are justifiably confident that Black will unearth a startling winning resource.

Black played the surprising move 1 . . . NxP!, whereupon White reacted even more surprisingly by resigning.

Actually, when we look into the situation more closely, we find there is no real reason for surprise. For example, if White plays 2 NxN, Black replies 2 . . . P—R6 and this Pawn cannot be prevented from queening!

Another plausible continuation is the following:

| WHITE | BLACK |
|---|---|
| 1 . . . . | NxP! |
| 2 N/K3—B1 | P—R6 |
| 3 K—B1 | . . . . |

Now Black can win a piece with 3 . . . P—R7. Instead, *he simplifies by exchanging*—still keeping the win of the piece in reserve.

| | |
|---|---|
| 3 . . . . | N—K6! |

This demonstrates the power of the passed Pawn. In the event of 4 NxN?? Black has 4 . . . P—R7 followed by the forced queening of the Pawn.

| 4 K—N2 | NxN |
| 5 NxN | P—R7 |
| 6 NxP | . . . . |

Clearly White has no choice. He must give up his Knight for the Pawn.

6 ....      BxN

And with a Bishop to the good, Black will win without any difficulty. Again the passed Pawn has demonstrated its power.

In Diagram 118 the position is so simplified that to the uninitiated eye it might seem barren of possibilities.

**BLACK**

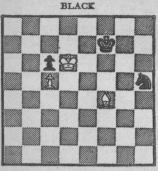

DIAGRAM 118
(White to play)
Where should White
move his attacked
Bishop?

**WHITE**

Actually White has a fairly easy win: he must win Black's Pawn, after which he can queen his own Pawn with very little effort. But first he must assure the safety of his Bishop.

| WHITE | BLACK |
|---|---|
| 1 B–K5! | .... |

After this Black might just as well resign, as his Knight cannot move. If, for example, he tries 1 . . . N–B3 there follows 2 BxN, KxB; 3 KxP and White queens his Pawn very quickly.

| 1 .... | K–K1 |
|---|---|
| 2 KxP | K–K2 |
| 3 K–N7 | K–K3 |
| 4 P–B6! | .... |

The passed Pawn is irresistible.

| 4 .... | KxB |
|---|---|
| 5 P–B7 | Resigns |

For the Pawn must queen.

When each player possesses a passed Pawn the result will depend on precision and timing. This is neatly illustrated in Diagram 119 (as well as in an earlier example—Diagram 115).

**BLACK**

**WHITE**

DIAGRAM 119
(Black to play)
Who has the stronger
passed Pawn?

White has a passed King Pawn, Black has a passed King Bishop Pawn. Both look formidable.

It is easy to jump to the conclusion that the King Pawn is the more useful of the two. The short-stepping Knight cannot afford to get too far away from the King Pawn, as this would enable the Pawn to march down to the queening square.

On the other hand, White seems well situated to hold back the Queen Bishop Pawn, as both his King and his Bishop command the queening square. Actually this turns out to be a faulty impression, for Black's Knight is fantastically agile.

| WHITE | BLACK |
|-------|-------|
| 1 .... | N—B6! |

This looks like a daredevil move, as White's King Pawn can now advance. But here is what would happen: 2 P—K6, P—B7ch; 3 K—B1, N—Q5!; 4 P—K7, N—K7ch; 5 K—N2, P—B8/Qch and Black has queened first after all.

The purpose of 1 . . . N—B6!, by the way, is to prevent White's King from going to King 1. Paradoxically, it is on Queen Bishop 1 that the King is more vulnerable.

2   B—B5      . . . .

The "safe" move 2 B—B1?? would not do at all because of the devastating reply 2 . . . P—B7 mate.

| 2 | . . . . | P—B7ch |
|---|---------|--------|
| 3 | K—B1    | N—Q7!  |
|   | Resigns |        |

White has no good defense against the coming . . . N—N6, which enforces the queening of the Pawn.

For example, after 4 K—N2 Black wins with 4 . . . N—N6; 5 KxN, P—B8/Q.

Or if White tries 4 B—K3, there follows 4 . . . KxB; 5 KxP, N—K5. In that case Black wins easily, as his Knight stops White's King Pawn in time and . . . KxBP makes it possible for Black's remaining Pawn to advance to the queening square.

This exciting endgame gives us a good inkling of the precision that is required when both sides have assets in the form of well-advanced passed Pawns.

The player of the Black pieces in this ending was Aron Nimzovich (1886-1935), probably the most original player in the history of the game and in some ways undoubtedly the most eccentric. His famous book, *My System,* went counter to so many accepted theories that it has not been fully accepted to this day, although it was first published in 1925.

Many are the anecdotes—and legends—that have flourished about this strange figure. The best of these stories relates to his hatred of smoking. On one occasion during an important tournament Dr. Vidmar playfully placed his cigar case, full of cigars, on the playing table. Though Vidmar showed no sign of wanting to smoke, Nimzovich was greatly agitated. Finally, unable to control himself any longer, he ran off to the tournament director with his complaint.

Trying to soothe him, the tournament director pointed out that Vidmar was not actually smoking. "Yes, that's true," Nimzovich answered, "but he might! And you know that in chess, the threat is stronger than the fulfillment!"

If Nimzovich was the genius of eccentricity, then Johannes Hermann Zukertort (1842-1888) was the genius of versatility. Though Zukertort had a degree in medicine from the University of Breslau, chess was his first love and he does not seem to have ever practiced medicine. His linguistic skill was fantastic, for he had a fluent grasp of Polish, English, Italian, Spanish, Latin, Greek, Hebrew, and Russian. He was also well versed in Turkish, Arabic, and Sanskrit.

But this was by no means all. He was a splendid **domino**

and whist player and, what is perhaps even more remarkable, an outstanding fencer and pistol shot. He fought with such distinction in the Prussian wars against Schleswig-Holstein, Austria, and France that he was awarded nine medals for bravery.

And we are still not at the end of Zukertort's versatility. He was equally at home in writing on such subjects as music, science, philology, theology, and prison reform.

But what about Zukertort as a chess player? He was one of the great masters of the age, second only to the seemingly unbeatable Steinitz. As a blindfold player he was second to none, and to play twenty such games at once did not trouble him unduly.

In Diagram 120 we see Zukertort at his imaginative and precise best. The endgame illustrates the queening power of a passed Pawn, but with what a power of rich creative detail!

BLACK

WHITE

DIAGRAM 120
(White to play)
How does White
exploit the power of his
far-advanced passed
Pawn?

White's passed Pawn on Queen Bishop 7 is his most powerful asset. Yet Black is just on the point of capturing it. Fragile as this Pawn looks, White (Zukertort) knows how to puts its massive power to the best use.

| WHITE | BLACK |
|---|---|
| 1  Q—N5!!! | . . . . |

Magnificent play, which not only attacks Black's Queen but also threatens 2 P—B8/Qch as well. Thus on 1 . . . K—Q2 Black's Queen is still pinned, so that White can come out a

Queen ahead (and more) with 2 P—B8/Qch, KxQ; 3 QxQch —or he can even win with 2 QxQch, KxQ; 3 P—B8/Qch.

|   |   |   |   |
|---|---|---|---|
| 1 | . . . . | | QxQ |

Black resigns himself to the inevitable.

|   |   |   |   |
|---|---|---|---|
| 2 | P—B8/Qch | | . . . . |

A neat point here is that after 2 . . . N—Q1 White forks King and Queen with 3 N—B7ch.

|   |   |   |
|---|---|---|
| 2 | . . . . | K—B2 |
| 3 | QxNch! | . . . . |

The new Queen immediately disappears from the board— but for a very good reason.

|   |   |   |
|---|---|---|
| 3 | . . . . | KxQ |
| 4 | N—B7ch | Resigns |

The Knight fork wins Black's Queen, so that White comes out a piece ahead as a result of his glorious combination.

White's winning method admirably combines the main theme of this chapter—Pawn promotion—with one of the themes of Chapter 2—the Knight fork as a winning pattern.

This makes a good point to conclude our study of the elements of chess—the mating patterns and other winning patterns in Chapter 2; the importance of rapid and effective development in Chapter 3; and Pawn promotion as the basic theme of Chapter 4. Armed with the knowledge you have thus acquired, you can look forward with confidence to playing successfully against opponents on your own level of experience and playing strength.

A final word of advice: If you have the time and the inclination, by all means continue your study of the game in order to improve your skill and enhance your enjoyment of chess. The goal of perfection eludes every player—even the World Champion; and therein lies the mysterious and inexhaustible charm of chess.

# SOLUTIONS TO QUIZ PROBLEMS

A (p. 55). White cannot play 1 QxBP mate because Black replies 1 . . . BxQ.

B (p. 56). Black reacts to 1 Q—R5ch with 1 . . . PxQ.

C (p. 60). If White plays 4 K—N1 we get our familiar pattern with 4 . . . RxN mate.

D (p. 62). 1 QxRP mate isn't feasible because of 1 . . . NxQ.

E (p. 63). In the event of 1 . . . K—N2 White replies 2 Q—R6 mate.

F (p. 66). White threatens 2 QxRP mate.

G (p. 69). It would be a mistake for White to play 1 N—B6ch, K—R1; 2 QxB because of the reply 2 . . . QxR mate.

H (p. 73). After 1 . . . K—N1 White plays 2 R/R7xPch, K—B1; 3 R/B7—B7 mate or 2 . . . K—R1; 3 Q—R5 mate.

I (p. 74). Black's Queen is taking an active part in the attack, whereas White's Queen is completely out of play.

J (p. 77). If White plays 1 R—K4, Black saves himself with 1 . . . Q—B1.

K (p. 83). White wins by a deadly discovered check, namely 1 P—Q6 dis ch, winning Black's Queen.

L (p. 96). By moving the Knight White prevents 4 . . . N—N5, which can be answered by 5 QxN.

M (p. 99). Black must not play 8 . . . QxNP because of 9 NxBPch forking Black's King and Rook.

N (p. 103). After 8 . . . Q—R3 or 8 . . . Q—N4 White plays 9 BxQ. After 8 . . . QxKP or 8 . . . QxNP White replies 9 NxQ.

O (p. 105). 3 QxP gives Black an opportunity to counter advantageously with 3 . . . N—QB3.

P (p. 106). 4 . . . P—KN3 is unsatisfactory for Black because of 5 QxKPch winning a Rook.

Q (p. 106). 6 . . . K—N3 is not feasible because White plays 7 Q—KB5 mate.

R (p. 106). 10 . . . Q—B3 blocks White's checkmate threat because it prevents a later B—K6 mate.

S (p. 107). Black must not play 11 . . . QxB?? because of the reply 12 Q–N5 mate.

T (p. 108). If Black plays 15 . . . Q–R5, White mates in two moves by 16 N–N3ch, K–N5; 17 B–K6 mate.

U (p. 110). If Black plays 8 . . . P–K4 White must not play 9 NxN?, for then Black wins a piece by 9 . . . QxBch.

V (p. 110). If Black plays 9 . . . QxP?? White plays 10 N–N5 with the threat of 10 B–B1 winning Black's Queen, and 10 N–B7ch winning a Black Rook.

W (p. 111). Black's Queen is trapped, for if 12 . . . QxRP; 13 RxQ. If 12 . . . Q–B4 or . . . Q–N7; 13 NxQ. If 12 . . . Q–N5 or . . . Q–B6 or . . . Q–K6; 13 BxQ. And if 12 . . . QxN; 13 QxQ.

X (p. 118). 11 . . . BxP wouldn't win material because the continuation 12 NxB, QxN; 13 B–N5ch would win Black's Queen.

Y (p. 119). 15 . . . P–QB3? is an altogether unsatisfactory reply because of 16 QxQ and Black cannot capture White's Queen.

Z (p. 119). If Black plays 18 . . . Q–B3 White wins the Black Queen by 19 RxQBP dis ch or 19 R–K6 dis ch. If Black plays 18 . . . Q–B5 White wins the Black Queen with 19 RxQBP dis ch or 19 R–K4 dis ch.

AA (p. 120). White's chief threat is 20 QxBP mate.

BB (p. 120). In the event of 20 . . . K–K1 White replies 21 Q–Q7 mate.